Lucy in the Afternoon

AN INTIMATE MEMOIR
OF LUCILLE BALL

Jim Brochu

G.K. HALL &CO.
Boston, Massachusetts
1991

Published in Large Print by arrangement with
William Morrow and Company, Inc.

British Commonwealth Rights Courtesy of
International Creative Management, Inc.

Grateful acknowledgment is made to Robert Osborne, columnist-critic of *The Hollywood Reporter*, for permission to quote from his tribute to Lucille Ball.

G. K. Hall Large Print Book Series.

Set in 18 pt. Plantin.

Library of Congress Cataloging-in-Publication Data

Brochu, Jim.
  Lucy in the afternoon : an intimate memoir of Lucille Ball / Jim
Brochu.
     p.   cm.—(G.K. Hall large print book series)
  Includes index.
  ISBN 0-8161-5077-X
  1. Ball, Lucille, 1911–1989.   2. Entertainers—United States—
Biography.   3. Large type books.   I. Title.
  [PN2287.B16B7   1991]
  791.45′028′092—dc20
  [B]   90-19934

*This book is dedicated to
the memory of
Desirée "DeDe" Hunt Ball,
Lucille's first fan.*

Introduction

FOR AS LONG as I can remember, I've had a recurring dream. The dream is that I'm in the subway, at the BMT Times Square Station, waiting for the uptown express. As I wait, I stroll down the platform and run into the pope, who is in full papal robes and reading the *New York Post*. He asks me where I'm headed, and I tell him I'm going to a party at Lucille Ball's house. I tell him she'd be thrilled if he came along. Won't he join me? He accepts.

We get into the subway car together, and after a short ride pull up in front of Lucy's house in Beverly Hills. The pope blesses the conductor and comments about the excellent transportation system we have in America as we walk up the driveway. Lucy answers the door herself, looks us up and down, and says, "What took you so long? Come on in." It was one dream I always wanted to come true.

A friend of mine who knew Lucie Arnaz

1

once told me about the incredible afternoon he got to spend with Lucille Ball at her house. As he talked about playing backgammon with her and sipping lemonade, I experienced rock-hard jealousy deep in the pit of my stomach for the first time in my life. As he went on, I kept thinking, It should have been me in that house playing with Lucy, not him. He didn't watch *I Love Lucy* twice a day. He didn't know every line of every episode by heart. He wasn't a "Lucy freak." He wasn't her biggest fan. How could this be happening?

As he rattled on about what Lucy was like at home, I seethed with a smile on my face. Indeed, life was unjust, and nothing would ever be right with the world again . . . until ten years later when Lucy and I became friends and we spent almost all our afternoons together.

As we played backgammon, we talked about everything. Lucy pulled no punches as she told me about her childhood, career, marriages, loves, hates, children, friends, successes, and failures. We talked about philosophy and gossiped like schoolchildren at recess, but most of all we laughed. Lucy loved to laugh.

After our visits, I would note down what

we chatted about, as well as any funny incidents that happened during the course of the day. This book is the story of Lucille Ball as she told it to me over a backgammon board between August 15, 1988, and April 17, 1989—her last day at home. I've written it for the millions of other people who each consider themselves to be Lucy's biggest fan, and for the many others who have said to me since her death—"I always dreamed of meeting her. You're so lucky. I wish I had been there."

CHAPTER
One

MY FIRST ENCOUNTER with Lucille Ball came in 1960, when I was fourteen years old. The minute I read in the Sunday paper that Lucy was coming to Broadway in a musical called *Wildcat*, I begged my father to get tickets. A few weeks later, we made the exciting trip over the Brooklyn Bridge to the Alvin Theatre on West Fifty-second Street for a Saturday matinee.

Even at that age, I was an admitted *I Love Lucy* freak. I not only watched every episode many times over, I studied them—especially

3

Lucy. Her timing, gestures, movements, glances, and line readings were lessons in how to do comedy. She was the master, and soon she would be standing in front of me live and in person.

Lucy made her entrance by crawling out from under a tin lizzie, her face smudged, cursing a mile a minute. Something was different about her, and it wasn't until halfway through the first act that I realized what it was. She was in color! God, was her hair red.

Lucy's performance was dazzling, and her energy was incredible . . . it was Lucy Ricardo in the Old West. I didn't want to leave after it was over, and waited around the back of the theater, hoping to catch a glimpse of Lucy. Suddenly, she floated across the darkened stage in an aqua-blue chiffon dressing gown. I charged down the aisle to intercept her, with my program held out like a lance. Lucy was unaware of me until I hit the orchestra pit rail at seventy miles an hour and moaned as I knocked the wind out of myself. It's a miracle I didn't flip right over the rail and into the drums.

I thrust my program out to her, but she just kept walking. She said, "Sorry, no autographs today," and disappeared into the wings. I was disappointed she didn't sign my playbill, but happy I could go back to school on Monday and tell everyone I met Lucy.

Eighteen years later, Sherwood Oaks Experimental College in Hollywood offered a six-week seminar in comedy to be taught by Lucille Ball. I signed up an hour later, and waited for the first Wednesday night class to begin. I walked up the stairs of an old building at the corner of Ivar Avenue and Hollywood Boulevard, looking forward to my intimate classes with the doyenne of the double take. I brought an apple and put it on her desk. When I turned to find a seat, I was shocked to see my "intimate class" had a hundred people in it. By the time I found a seat, there were a half-dozen apples on the desk along with mine.

The dean of the college announced that the first class would begin by showing Lucy's favorite *I Love Lucy* episode, the one where she meets William Holden at the Brown Derby and dumps a plate of spaghetti on his head. After the screening, Lucy walked to the front of the classroom and we stood in unison, cheering her. She put up her hands to quiet the group and said, "If you act this way, I'll have to keep you after class." The ovation got louder.

Lucy turned to the desk, saw the apples,

and scanned the room. "What sons of a bitches put the apples there?" Twenty people raised their hands. "It won't do you any good," she growled. "I don't give out grades." She lit a cigarette and climbed into the tall director's chair. "I have nothing to say," she began. "What you get out of this class is up to you. It all depends on what you bring to it. You have to ask questions. That's the only way I can teach."

The six weeks that followed were classes not only in comedy but in life. The one point Lucy stressed over and over again was what she called the key to her own success. "Say yes to everything. Do everything you're asked to do without complaining. Learn something new about your trade every day. Study hard, and work harder."

Lucy felt there was a lot of luck involved with her own success. "I landed in Hollywood on a scholarship," she told us. "I was being paid to be in movies. Sure, they were chorus and bit parts, but all the time, I was watching and learning. I was like a sponge soaking up everything I could, and they were paying me to do it."

She chain-puffed on her cigarette as she answered the first volley of questions from the class, "Did Fred and Ethel really hate each other offscreen?" "Why did you and Desi get divorced?" "Is your son really on drugs?" "Does your daughter sleep around?" Lucy answered all questions with embarrassing honesty.

After a few weeks, the class thinned out to those who really wanted to study comedy with her. One of the students was a well-known young black actress who had once been a stand-up comedian and went on to play a lead on a then-popular TV sitcom. In class, she would always try to monopolize Lucy's time with inane questions prefaced —to impress the rest of us unknowns—with who she was and where she was currently appearing.

Lucy was cool but polite to her at first, but after a while she'd had it with the prima donna and blasted her. "Who the hell do you think you are?" Lucy shouted. The room fell chillingly silent. Lucy rose out of her director's chair like Marshal Dillon headed for the showdown. She squared off with the actress. "You know something, you're a lucky girl. You have no talent. I've seen you. You're a loud-mouth show-off who'll be here today and gone tomorrow. Now sit down and shut up, and let one of these kids get a word in edgeways!" I thought the girl would walk out, but she did sit down and she did shut up.

Lucy was asked a strange question: "Miss Ball, do you still have any wishes that haven't come true?" She said, "Only one. I don't want to live to be as old as my mother. It would be very tough not to be physical." Lucy's mother, DeDe (short for Desirée), was eighty-five when she died only a few months before our classes began.

When the six weeks ended, Lucy wished us all well. The students mobbed her for autographs as she left the class, and I thought about the day at the Alvin Theatre when she turned me down. So I stood on line with the rest of the class to ask Lucy to sign my notebook. Just as I got to the front, her driver pulled her away, saying she would be late for her next appointment. I still had no autograph.

Ten years later, I wrote a play called *The Lucky O'Learys*, about a woman who schemes to win the biggest lottery in American history. I thought it would be perfect for my former teacher. I called around town to see if anyone had her home address, and I couldn't get it. I walked down to Hollywood Boulevard, about a block from where I had studied with her, and bought a map to the stars' homes. I found her address and sent her the play. With it, I wrote a note reminding her of the Sherwood Oaks classes, and closed by challenging her to a game of backgammon.

Two days later, I received a call from Gary Morton. "Lucy read the script," he said, "and she loved it. She thinks it's sensational." My heart leapt. Gary continued, "But she doesn't think it's right for her." My heart dropped. "Do you have any other ideas for her? She wants to wear nice clothes. I want her to do a remake of the *Solid Gold Cadillac*, but she loved Judy Holliday in the movie and the lady who did it on Broadway . . ."

"Josephine Hull?"

"That's right. She doesn't think she can top them."

"I think she could top anybody," I said.

"I agree. Anyway, Lucy would like to meet you for a game of backgammon." (My heart leapt again.) "Can you come over to the house some afternoon?"

I told him I was available anytime. Gary said they were leaving for New York in a few days and would call when they got back. Lucy never made it to New York. On May 10, 1988, shortly after our conversation, she was rushed to Cedars-Sinai with a stroke and a minor heart attack.

Despite the fact that her condition was serious, Lucy checked herself out of the hospital after a few days to recuperate at home. I sent a get-well card to her almost every day. She saved them all, including one in which I wrote her a limerick. It went:

> You woke one morning "sans
>   stamina,"
> So you had the doctor examine ya.
> He said, "Go home please,
> You're just weak in the knees."
> So I'm gonna come over and
>   gammon ya.

The day she returned home, I splurged and sent her two hundred roses along with a card saying, "This phony illness is not going to make me take pity on you and let you win. I will throttle you at the game table."

A few days later, I received a note. It read:

Dear Jim,
    Ten dozen roses? No wonder you're anxious to get even. I really appreciated hearing from you . . . felt for a while as

though I was leaving town without having a chance to get out. Let Wanda [her secretary] know when you're available. Bring money and credit cards because I play for a whole dollar and sometimes double the cube twice.

Love,
Lucy.

I called Wanda immediately and said, "I'm available!" She told me that Lucy was feeling better but wasn't up to having visitors yet. She would call me when the doctor said it was okay.

After a few weeks, the phone rang. It was Wanda. "Hi, Jim. Lucille Ball is calling you. I'm going to put you through to the house. Speak up. Sometimes it's a bad connection." Before I could thank her, she put me on hold. As I waited, I practiced saying hello at a few different volumes. I wanted to be loud without being heard in Tibet. The phone clicked, and she spoke. "Hi!" she said. "I guess we should finally meet."

"Absolutely," I replied. "Your place or mine?"

She laughed. "What are you doing this afternoon?"

"I'm coming to see you."

"Good. Two o'clock?"

"Perfect."

"See you then," I said cheerfully. When I hung up, my hand was shaking.

I was like a teenage boy trying to pick out the right tie for my first date. I tore my closet apart but couldn't find anything to wear. I saw one of my favorite shirts in the hamper. It was filthy. I thought if I washed it immediately, it would be dry in time for my meeting with Lucy.

Wrong. A few hours later, I walked up the driveway, not sure if the clammy feeling up and down my back was nerves or my wet shirt. As I looked up at Lucy's house, I thought my recurring dream was coming true. I was going to Lucy's house, and she was waiting for me inside. The only thing missing was the pope. I rang the doorbell and then saw the sign: BEWARE OF DOG I could hear the yapping of the approaching monster hound. In an instant, the door was open and the dog was at my heels, barking and humping my leg.

I looked down and saw Tinker, a two-pound white toy poodle that found love at first sight with my right leg. I looked up and saw a lady holding the door open; a rotund little woman in a white lab coat. She looked like an igloo on orthopedic oxfords. She seemed to know who I was. "Jim? Come on in. Lucy's expecting you. I'm her nurse, Trudi Arcudi." It sounded like a new series to me—*Trudi Arcudi, Private Duty*. I entered the house, dragging the dog behind me. She was still yapping and making love to my right shin.

"Down, Tinker, down!" came the voice. It scared me so much *I* almost got down. Tinker ceased immediately. I looked up and saw Lucy. She was dressed in white sandals, white slacks, white blouse, white scarf, and carried a big white purse. I looked her up and down and said, "You look like a big dish of vanilla yogurt." She chuckled.

"So I was your teacher, eh?" she said.

"You sure were. Do you remember me?"

She studied my face and shook her head. "Nope! Tell me what you learned."

I blanked. "I can't remember my name right now, and you want me to know what I learned. I do remember the night you blasted that TV actress."

"Yeah? I blasted her in private, too."

"What do you mean?" I asked.

Lucy made a face and said, "Just the sight of her made me sick. I called her into one of the offices after that class and told her to

13

either stop showing off or stop showing up. She chose the latter. Now, she's back on the air in that lousy show. What does it all mean?"

"Well," I said philosophically, "as the great Albert Einstein once said . . . go figure!"

She laughed. "You're funny." I felt as if I had been knighted by the queen.

We walked through the house and into the backyard. At the end of the long emerald-green lawn was the pool, and behind that a small white house. We walked along the brick path, passed the guest house (where Orson Welles lived at one time), the billiard room (which was now overrun with mementos, magazine clippings, and pictures), and on into the little white pool house.

A white backgammon table and four chairs sat in the corner. The walls were covered with photographs from *Mame;* over fifty rehearsal and production stills.

"I love this room," she said, "but I never get out here. Well, sit down and let's go! I'm feeling lucky."

What followed was one of the most embarrassing moments of my life. I sat down in the yellow leather chair opposite Lucy and broke it. Neither she nor Trudi heard the crunch, so I wondered if I should admit it now and get thrown out, or wait until later and get thrown out. I decided to get it over with.

"I don't know how to tell you this," I started, "but I just broke your chair."

She looked surprised. "How did you do that?"

"I sat on it."

She was smiling. "Don't worry about it. Take that chair." I took a matching chair from the other side of the table, sat down, and *broke that one, too!* This time the crunch echoed throughout the room.

"Jesus!" she said. "Did you break that one, too?"

"I did. Maybe I should stand."

"I only have a few left," she said.

I took a high-backed chair from a corner and placed it at the table. "This one looks sturdy."

She looked at me suspiciously. "The other ones looked sturdy, too." I knew she was thinking, What have I gotten myself into?

We started playing right away. We talked as we played, and discovered we had some things in common. My mother died when I was three, the same age as Lucy when her father died. We were both born in New York

State. We were both Leos. I told her my birthday was the next day, and she was allowed to give me lots of presents. She grunted, "Maybe I'll give you a chair."

After an hour, we both felt very comfortable with each other. She was easy to be with, and very down-to-earth. She suddenly thought about a joke Gary had told her that day. The actual joke was about two little kids who were discussing politics. The boy says to the girl, "I'll show you my Dukakis if you show me your Bush." Lucy thought it was a very funny story, and couldn't wait to try it out on someone. Me!

She began the joke correctly about the two kids, and then she took a wrong turn into politics, Democrats, elephants, elections, and conventions. Then, a light bulb went off in her head as she finally remembered the punch line. (Or thought she did.) "I know. I know," she said, sitting up straight. "If you show me your Dukakis, I'll show you my pussy!"

Trudi turned as white as her lab coat. "What?"

My mouth fell completely open.

Lucy looked at us blankly. "Isn't that funny?"

I took a chance and said, "I don't know.

16

I've never seen your pussy. I don't know if it's funny or not." With that, Lucy realized what she had said and howled. The three of us laughed for ten minutes. She wiped the mascara as it ran down her face. "Oh God, did I really say that?"

I shook my head and said, "Yes. You really said it. And by the way, I'm not really Jim Brochu. I'm from the *National Enquirer*, and that's going to be our headline for next week's edition . . . 'Lucille Ball's Genitals Resemble Democratic Frontrunner.'"

She howled again. "Stop it. Stop it." It was at that moment that I knew Lucy loved to laugh. She was a great audience, and to her a long guffaw was as powerful as any prescription medicine. When Gary came home a few hours later, we told him how Lucy had screwed up the joke, and the four of us laughed all over again.

We had been playing about four hours on that first day when she had to get ready for dinner. The score was 17–16. I beat her by one point and won a dollar. "I had a wonderful day, Lucy. I'm sorry you lost money."

"I don't need your money," she said as she handed me the bill, "I need your friendship."

I took the dollar. "Thank you, Lucy. I'll always remember today."

"Me, too. What are you doing tomorrow?"

"I hope I'm coming to see you again," I said.

She winked. "Two o'clock?"

"I'll be here." I gave her a kiss on the cheek and started down the brick pathway back to the house. Lucy called after me, "Drive carefully!"

"I will."

"Hey! One more thing!" she shouted.

"What?"

"Don't break any more chairs!"

CHAPTER
Two

THE NEXT DAY was my forty-second birthday. As I drove the eight miles over Coldwater Canyon from my house in the San Fernando Valley, I thought about being another year older and flashed on an *I Love Lucy* episode. Lucy Ricardo was giving an interview to a woman's magazine, and the reporter asked her, "When's your birthday?"

Lucy used her own birthday. "August sixth," she replied sweetly.

The interviewer probed further. "August sixth . . . what?"

"August sixth. Period," answered Lucy tersely.

Spending my birthday with Lucy was the best present I could have been given. I learned my lesson from the Sherwood Oaks classes and came with a mental list of things I wanted to ask her about. I came around to the side door (as I had been told to do) and rang. Frank Gorey opened the door.

Frank is a transplanted New Yorker in his early sixties, a staunch Democrat and a devout Catholic. He worked for Lucy almost thirty years as her houseman, driver, appointment-maker, and majordomo. He always joked that he was going to write a book one day called *Being Frank With Lucy*.

Lucy was waiting for me in the den. She was dressed all in white again, exactly the same outfit as the day before. Lucy had a new gown designed for almost every public appearance she made, but while she was in her own home, I never saw her in more then ten different outfits.

Lucy was visiting with an elderly gentleman whom she introduced to me as Hal

King. Hal and Lucy were celebrating fifty years of friendship. They met shortly after she moved to Los Angeles from New York and he from Chicago. They used to go roller-skating and horseback riding together, and at one time even talked about getting married. Both of their mothers were pushing them into it, thinking it would be a match made in heaven, but Lucy and Hal decided they would rather remain good friends.

Hal was from a wealthy steel family, one of nine children. One of his sisters married the makeup mogul Max Factor, and another married Max's brother Joe. Max brought Hal into the business, and he served as Lucy's personal makeup man from the mid-forties until he retired in 1976. Even though Hal did Lucy's makeup from the very first episode of *I Love Lucy* (and was paid well for it), Max Factor demanded and got on-screen credit until Hal's contract with him expired in 1955.

At first I thought Hal was a little strange, since he was wearing a heavy sweater over a wool shirt in the middle of a very hot August afternoon. I later found out that Hal isn't strange, just constantly cold. Lucy, Trudi, Hal, and I walked out to the pool house once again, where I sat without breaking a chair.

We repeated Lucy's Dukakis-Bush blooper to Hal, which set us off laughing for five minutes. It was like watching a good rerun.

Hal asked Lucy how she was feeling since the stroke. I noticed an exchange of looks between Lucy and nurse Trudi when the subject of the stroke was mentioned. Gary tried to keep it out of the papers by telling the press that Lucy had suffered only a mild heart attack. But the fact is that she did have a stroke on May 10, and it was serious. She told us how it happened.

Lucy said, "I woke up about four-thirty in the morning and went to the bathroom. I didn't turn any lights on, since I knew my way in the dark, and sat down on the toilet. After a minute, I felt this heavy object crash into my lap. I thought a piece of the ceiling fell down, it hit me so hard. I reached into my lap to see what it was and almost screamed when I found an arm there. My own right arm! It had fallen asleep. It was over my head when I got up, and I never felt it or thought anything was wrong until it fell in my lap. What a scary feeling that is . . . to find a dead arm in your lap and then realize it's yours. I started back to bed, but fell before I got there. Gary picked me up and took me to Cedars. God, I hate that

21

hospital. Please don't ever let me die at Cedars. [She did.] Anyway, they had me in intensive care, and I don't know what they gave me, but all of a sudden I was hallucinating. I started seeing cockroaches marching up and down my stomach; parading all over me to "Seventy-Six Trombones." I started screaming, and they strapped me down. I yelled, 'Get me out of this goddamned place. I want to go home.' I didn't know it, but I was right under a microphone connected to the nurses' station, and so my screams were going all over the hospital. Well, at least they heard me. I was out of there in a few hours. I didn't care if I died as long as I got out of that damn place. God, I hate hospitals."

Trudi told us that Lucy's recovery had been remarkable. Her right side had been partially paralyzed, and a weaker person would not have come through it. Lucy wanted to get back in shape, although she insisted that she had nothing to get back in shape for. She walked with Gary every morning and worked out with her friend Onna White as often as she could. Three months after the stroke, she was almost fully recovered except that she drooled slightly out of the left corner of her mouth and tired easily. Both of those aftereffects cleared up a few weeks later.

"I hate being sick," she protested. "I was never sick before in my life." (Although over the forthcoming days, she told me about the many illnesses she'd had since childhood.)

"You know when the beginning of the end was?" she asked me.

"When?"

"*Stone Pillow*. I *never* recovered from that."

Stone Pillow was a 1985 made-for-television movie in which Lucy played a bag lady named Florabelle. The movie was to be shot entirely on location in New York City. Since the story took place in winter, Lucy had to wear layers and layers of heavy clothing. (The Hal King look.) Producer Merrill Karpf decided to shoot in March to take advantage of the cooler temperatures, but what they got instead was a record heat wave.

Lucy, being the trouper she was, continued to do scene after scene in 90-degree heat. The result was a two-week hospital stay; the diagnosis, dehydration. In a woman of Lucy's age, seventy-four at the time, dehydration is a debilitating condition that weakens all the major organs. It was during this time that the doctors ordered Lucy to quit smoking. They discovered she was allergic to cigarettes. Although she constantly puffed on cigarettes from the time she was eighteen years old, she swore she never inhaled. I flashed back to my classes with her and re-membered she chain-smoked the entire six weeks.

She told Hal and me that *Stone Pillow* was a grueling experience. She had looked for-ward to working with Rose Goldemberg (the author) and George Schaefer (the director), but things didn't work out as she had hoped. Because of a personal tragedy, Mrs. Goldem-berg could not do the badly needed rewrites, and Lucy, as she was with so many of her directors, was disappointed with George Schaefer's work. Lucy got angry thinking about the man. "He didn't direct. His title should have been suggestor. I asked him for help, but he never gave it to me. I think there was too much of 'Lucy' in Florabelle, and I was trying to prevent that. I didn't know how to do it on my own, and he didn't, either."

She thought about the shooting of the film. "You know what was strange?" she asked. "When I was in those bag-lady clothes . . . nobody would look at me. Peo-ple would stop when they saw the camera and the lights and all the people, and they'd ask me what was going on, but they would never look at me." She started laughing as she continued, "Except for the guy who did one of the greatest takes I've ever seen. I was coming down the street in my costume to go home for the day. My car was waiting around the corner from the shoot. This very nice-looking advertising kind of guy came down the street and saw me and he smiled, and without my asking him for it, he reached into his wallet and handed me five dollars. I took the bill from him and stepped into the waiting limousine, and I thought his head would snap off his shoulders. Jesus, what a double take. I got out of the car and told him who I was, and then—and here's the best part—he thought he was on *Candid Camera*. When I told him he wasn't, he asked for his five dollars back. God, it was hot!"

After we'd played backgammon for a few hours, Lucy got up from the table and went to a corner of the room. Hal and Trudi exchanged looks, and I sat there wondering what was going on. Lucy turned around holding a plate on which was a hot-cross bun with a lit candle. She sang "Happy Birthday" to me in that low, offkey foghorn voice as she held out the plate and walked back over to the table. She put the bun down in front of me and kissed me on the cheek. "Make a wish!"

"I don't have to," I said. "It just came true." I blew out the candle anyway.

"Here," she said, handing me a small, shiny green gift box.

"You remembered."

"Well," she said, "you certainly reminded me enough!"

I opened the enclosed card and read it. "Happy, happy to a new friend. Love, Lucy." I opened the box. Inside was a gold watch with her famous caricature on the face and the inscription "Love, Lucy." I felt as if I had won the Irish Sweepstakes. I told her that she'd more than made up for the fact that she refused me an autograph at the Alvin Theatre some thirty years before. She had no idea what I was talking about, of course, but when I told her the whole story, she was genuinely upset about it. "I'm so sorry. But you have to do that sometimes. I'll make it up to you."

I told her she already had. The mention of *Wildcat* unleashed a flood of memories for her.

"Boy, that was a disaster! Everything went

wrong from the start. I knew the book was only so-so, but I wanted to do it because Jimmy Van Heusen and Sammy Cahn were going to do the score. Wouldn't you know, an hour after I signed the contract, they called to say they had a fight with Richard Nash [who wrote the book] and quit! Imagine . . . *one hour*. God! Desi produced the show, you know."

I didn't know. "I thought Michael Kidd and Nash were the producers," I said.

"Well," she said sarcastically, "their names were on the program as producers, but they didn't do much. When Cahn and Van Heusen dropped out, I called Desi, and he said Desilu would put up the money. He gave them five hundred thousand dollars on the spot, and we took a chance with Cy Coleman. He'd written a couple of hit songs, but he never wrote a score. I wrote, 'Hey, Look Me Over!' "

"Does Cy know that?"

"Well," she said sheepishly, "I didn't write it note for note, but I gave Cy the idea for it. I told him I wanted to beat the drum and tell people to look at me. He wrote the notes, but the idea was mine."

I asked her what the biggest problem with the show was. She answered quickly, "That nobody cared but me and the chorus kids. Nash didn't care. Kidd didn't. Neither of them gave a damn what they put on the stage because they thought people would come to see me no matter how bad the show was. I thought everything was okay until one of the kids in the chorus, Swen Swenson, came up to me and said, 'May I speak to you, Miss Ball?' I told him, 'Only if you call me Lucy.' He said that Michael Kidd was known for working his dancers into the ground by the difficulty of what they were called on to do, but in this show, no one had even broken a sweat. They were embarrassed by the slapdash effort he was making, and wanted to work. I told Kidd and Nash that I wasn't happy and they would have to do better. The next thing I hear going around town is that I'm a demanding monster who's impossible to work with."

"Do you think you're a perfectionist?"

She got very serious. "No. I know nothing is going to be perfect, but I want it to be the best it can be, and I want to see the people who are getting paid well because they're supposed to know what they're doing, doing it. You can still try for perfection even though you know you'll never achieve it."

28

"Are you still friends with Paula Stewart?"

"Sure. I see Paula all the time."

Paula played the part of Lucy's sister Janie in *Wildcat*. At the time, she was married to Jack Carter, and they introduced Lucy to a mutual friend named Gary Morton, who became Lucy's second husband.

Lucy continued, "It's funny that Paula even got the job."

"How do you mean?"

"I was sitting in the back of the theater one day during auditions, and this bimbo slithered up to me like she was doing a bad Marilyn Monroe impression. [Lucy went right into character, re-creating the girl's breathy voice.] 'Hi! I'm Sylvia, and do you want to hear something marvy? I'm playing your little sister.'

"Really? Oh no, you're not."

"But Mr. Kidd said I had the part."

"But Miss Ball says you don't."

She broke character and continued the story. "Jack Carter told me about his wife, Paula, and thought she might be right for the show. We met for dinner one night, and she looked perfect for the part. Petite and perky, blond, wholesome. I wanted to hear her sing. She came to the theater the next day to sing for Nash and Kidd—who wasn't pleased but so what—and me. She got two notes out of her mouth, and I yelled stop! Paula ran off the stage thinking she was terrible, but she was great. I didn't need to hear anymore. I knew she had the part in two notes."

Lucy looked through a souvenir book of the show I brought her and shook her head as she turned the pages. "There was a lot of bad luck connected with that show. Maybe I shouldn't have done it. I was running away from California. Maybe it was just an ego trip. Things don't usually work out if they're done just for ego trips. But I always wanted to do a show on Broadway. I was sick all through the run of it. [This from the woman who said she was never sick.] I fainted twice onstage. Once I was doing a scene with Edith King, a wonderful old character woman, and I started to pass out. I could feel myself going, and I grabbed her hand and broke her wrist. Poor thing was in a cast for three months.

"The other time I fainted, I was on the oil rig about twenty feet off the stage. If Keith hadn't caught me, I wouldn't be here."

Keith Andes, as Joe Dynamite, was Lucy's leading man in *Wildcat*, and appeared in several of her TV shows.

"Keith was a good guy," she continued. "He really stuck up for me. The night I fell off the rig, I got hysterical, and they called the house doctor and the son of a bitch wanted to inject me. I knew what he wanted to inject me with, and it was something I didn't want. He was trying to stab me with a hypodermic needle right through my costume. I was fighting this quack off—actually *fighting* him—when Keith heard what was going on, broke into the dressing room, and pulled the guy off me. I thought he was going to kill him." She shook her head. "Jeez, that was a lousy show."

"*I* liked it," I said.

"You were fourteen, you liked everything," she chuckled. "I wish we could have kept the show running for the kids' [in the chorus] sake. They worked so hard. I was just so sick. But we did break box-office records."

"For what?"

"We gave more ticket refunds than any show in the history of Broadway." She sighed. "I think I'd like to do a play. That would be fun. I miss being in front of an audience."

I said, "I'll write you a play."

"Okay."

It was getting late, and I wondered if I would be asked to come back a third day. I was—Lucy said, "I'm used to you now." After that, it was understood that I would come and play with her every day. That night, I decided to do all my work at night so every afternoon would be free for Lucy.

CHAPTER
Three

AFTER A FEW days of coming to the house, I was totally accepted by Lucy and those who worked for her. Lucy was not comfortable with the number of people on her staff, which included her driver, Frank Gorey; her cook and houseman, Roza and Chris, a married couple who had immigrated from Poland; Michael Maurer, Gary's nephew, who sat around the house watching television until he was called on to do an errand; and at the time, Trudi Arcudi, Lucy's nurse. "Isn't this ridiculous?" she said with disgust one day. "Five people to take care of two."

Lucy loved the Roxbury Drive house and knew she wanted to live in it the minute she saw it. She told me about the strange series of circumstances that led her to buy it.

Lucy and Desi were living on the ranch in Northridge when there was a kidnapping threat against the children in the early part of 1955. Both she and Desi felt that they were too far removed from any kind of protection living in the valley, and so they decided it was time to buy a place in town. There they would have people around them and the best police protection in the world. Strangers have been known to be stopped by the Beverly Hills police for just walking down the street.

Lucy began her search for a house in town. She was taken by a real estate broker to see many different properties, but none of them was "it." On one particular afternoon, the broker called her to say that she knew she'd found the ideal house for Lucy. It was on two lots at the corner of Roxbury Drive and Lexington Avenue, in the heart of Beverly Hills. The address was 1001.

Lucy looked at the house and liked it, but there was something that still didn't "feel right." It was an enormous house, a real Hollywood mansion that the broker told her was the perfect place for the king and queen of Hollywood. It wouldn't be on the market for long, and if Lucy wanted it, she should make an offer immediately. Lucy, trying to buy time, told her that Desi would have to see it before any offer could be made.

As Lucy and the broker left the house, Lucy looked across the street and saw the two-story white Williamsburg house at 1000 North Roxbury. She felt something come over her as she stared at the house; it reminded her of the houses she had admired as a child in the wealthy section of Jamestown, New York. She asked the broker if she could see that house, but the broker said it wasn't for sale. Besides, it wasn't a mansion . . . just a big house. Lucy didn't care. She wanted to see it.

She walked across the street and rang the bell. An elderly woman came to the door, and Lucy introduced herself. The name Lucille Ball made no impression on the woman, who had a sad and melancholy countenance. Lucy told her that she had seen the house from across the street, and wondered if the woman would ever consider selling the place.

The elderly lady's eyes widened as she told Lucy that she and her husband had discussed putting the house up for sale only the night before. She introduced herself as Mrs. Bang, and invited Lucy inside. "You should have seen the look on the real estate lady's face when I went in."

The moment Mrs. Bang closed the door behind Lucy, she burst into tears. Lucy was startled and looked around for help, but they were alone in the house. Mrs. Bang told Lucy that she and her husband had recently finished building a guest house in the back for their son, so he could have a place to live when he was discharged from the service. Just before the son was discharged, he had been killed in an accident. Now, every time Mr. or Mrs. Bang stepped into the backyard, they felt they were looking not at a guest house as much as a memorial to their dead son.

Lucy told Mrs. Bang that she'd fallen in love with the house from across the street, and when the old woman took her through the place, Lucy knew she had found the house of her dreams. When Mr. Bang came home, Lucy was still there. Earlier in the day, he had decided that he and his wife should sell and start over in a small apartment where they would not be confronted by the death of their only son whenever they opened a door.

Lucy made them an offer on the spot. Mr. Bang countered, and Lucy accepted. She would give them $85,500, a fair price considering that there would be no broker's fees to pay. (Gary Morton recently put the house on the market for $7.8 million.) When Lucy walked out the front door, an impatient and semi-irate real estate lady was cooling her heels on the front steps. "We can go now," Lucy told her. "I just bought a house." The broker countered icily, "I thought your husband had to see it first."

"That's all right," said Lucy. "I described it to him on the phone, and he loved it."

Lucy and Desi began renovations almost as soon as the escrow closed. The first thing they added was the lanai, the large den that became the center of the house where they spent most of their time. In the following months, they added an upstairs den over the lanai, the pool, pool house, cabanas, billiard room next to the garage, and an exercise/rehearsal room with a piano at one end and an exercise treadmill at the other. One more building was added to the grounds a few years ago; a 4' × 4' dollhouse built for Lucy's granddaughter, Kate Luckinbill. Gary joked that if they put the dollhouse on the empty lot down the block, they could get $2 million for it.

Lucy decorated the house herself. It's an eclectic assemblage of antiques: overstuffed chairs and comfortable sofas and items gathered from auctions. In every room was a backgammon table copied from the ones that Lucy used to play on at the now-defunct backgammon club Pips.

Shortly after Lucy and Desi bought the house, it was featured in an *I Love Lucy* episode. In the segment where Lucy and Ethel take a bus tour of the stars' Beverly Hills homes, they ask the driver to let them off in front of the house of Richard Widmark. This was actually Lucy's home, and the wall that she scales to pick a Widmark grapefruit was a replica of the white wall surrounding her corner property.

I always felt a sense of history whenever I walked in that side door, the same as a Jefferson historian might feel at the thrill of stepping into Monticello and being greeted by old Tom himself. On the left was the entrance to the large kitchen accented by its flowered wallpaper and yellow cabinets. Through the kitchen was a long hallway that led to a small breakfast room, an ironing room, and a storage room that had been turned into a functional beauty parlor where Irma Kusely would do Lucy's hair.

Continuing down the other hallway was the dining room on the right and Gary's den on the left. Except for the den, there were hardly any hints that the residents of the house were in show business. The den is a large room paneled in dark oak but mostly covered with memorabilia. Two red leather club chairs sat in front of a wall-length bookcase filled with videotapes of all of Lucy's shows and guest appearances. One section of the bookcase was reserved for kiddie videos for the visiting grandchildren, and on the top of another shelf was a complete set of Gary's favorite sitcom, *Fawlty Towers*.

At the far end of the room was a built-in fireplace over which hung three portraits. One of Lucie (at age seven), one of Desi, Jr. (at age five), and in the center, a large portrait of Lucy done by her friend Claire Trevor. It was one of Lucy's favorite pieces, although she always protested, "My nose is off. I look like Mighty Joe Young."

On the opposite wall was a large picture of Simon Luckinbill, Lucy's first grandchild, as a tiny, bare-bottomed baby. It was done up as a theater poster announcing his birth. "Mr. and Mrs. Laurence Luckinbill Present . . ." with Simon's date of birth, weight, and length. Under the poster was a large easy chair, and next to that a table with a framed, signed photo of their late next-door neighbor Jack Benny.

Next to the window that looked out onto Roxbury Drive was Gary's large oak desk. As I made a phone call one day, I was amazed to look out and see the number of cars that would slow down so the occupants could look or take pictures. One day, a stretch limousine stopped in front of the house and about twenty Japanese businessmen jumped out, all holding cameras, all madly clicking away. I called Lucy to come and look. "Jesus," she said as she watched an endless stream of people get out of the backseat, "it looks like a Japanese clown car."

One day as I was leaving the house, the sunset was particularly beautiful. Lucy stepped out to look at it with me. When she saw the street was quiet, she took my arm and we walked down the driveway to get a better view. Just out of sight was a minivan packed with a family who had parked to take videos of the house. Suddenly, they saw Lucy, and turned the camera on her. We could hear them screaming, "There she is! It's her. It's Lucy!" Lucy immediately put herself into reverse and walked backward up the driveway, waving and smiling at them while saying under her breath, "Oh God, please don't let them get out of the car." She made it safely back in the house before they rushed her. I called her when I got home and told her it was nice of her to wave and smile at them. She laughed. "If I didn't, they probably would have rushed the back door and stayed for dinner."

Across from the den was the dining room, also done in yellow, a simple room containing a large white Formica table, breakfront, sideboard, and potbelly stove. When we would have dinner there, Lucy would sit at the head of the table, with Gary facing her at the other end. Chris would serve the meals wearing black pants and white short-sleeved shirt, while *Wheel of Fortune* or *Jeopardy* kept us company in the background.

There was always a great deal of laughter at the table from trying to play along with the games or from Lucy's unintentional antics, which could have been taken from right out of one of her shows. Under her foot was a button that rang a bell in the kitchen to let Chris know he was needed in the dining room.

Nine out of ten times, Lucy would hit the bell accidentally and not realize it. Chris, who had not been with them long, would rush in through the swinging door, bowing in his best Continental style, and ask what was needed. Lucy looked up, surprised. "Nothing!"

Chris looked perplexed, but would back into the kitchen until Lucy hit the bell by accident again, then he would burst through the doors once more, eager to please. Lucy had no idea what we were laughing about until one time she stepped on the bell deliberately so Chris would clear the dishes. He didn't respond, thinking he had caught on to her accidental rings. Lucy finally yelled for him. When he appeared, she reprimanded him and said, "When I ring the bell, you should come in here!"

Chris was obviously confused. When we told Lucy she had been hitting the bell by accident, first she laughed and then she went into the kitchen to apologize to Chris for the mix-up.

The main entrance to the house was seldom used. I once told Lucy that the entrance hall to her house was the same size as an apartment I once had in Manhattan. To the right was a formal living room, and to the front, a grand staircase. The living room was never used. The walls were covered with fine paintings, the furniture exquisite, the drapes brocade, and the feeling cold and formal.

In one corner was a backgammon table (as usual), and behind the table a small bookcase filled with her original scripts bound into leather volumes. One hundred seventy-nine episodes of *I Love Lucy*, one hundred fifty-six of *The Lucy Show*, and one hundred forty-four of *Here's Lucy*. Four hundred seventy-nine half-hour episodes in all: almost two hundred forty hours of television.

Up the grand staircase and to the left was the master bedroom. A king-size bed covered by a green quilted bedspread dominated the room. Across from the bed was a glass-and-chrome bookcase holding a television and some of Lucy's favorite things: a picture of her when she was two years old, wide-eyed and thick-lipped, crowned with a big white bow in her dark curly hair. Two of her Emmys rested on the top shelf (two were in her New York apartment and the fifth in her house at Snowmass, Colorado.)

To the left was Gary's massive dressing room, and to the right was Lucy's famous pink bathroom, a gift from Gary while Lucy was away shooting *Mame*. The bathroom was enormous, and included a dressing table, two sinks, toilet, bidet, and a massive, square, sunken pink tub. Granddaughter Kate loved the bathtub more than anything else, and insisted her grandmother allow her long, luxurious soaks with every visit.

Across the hall from Lucy and Gary's bedroom were Little Lucie and Desi, Jr.'s suites, which had been overtaken as storage areas since the kids went out on their own. Lucy laughed as she showed me Desi, Jr.'s room. "The nights I spent up here tearing all the plugs out of the wall."

"What plugs?" I asked.

"Whenever we had to punish him, we'd send him to his room, until I realized that it was like sending him to Disneyland. He had a stereo, a television, a tape recorder, electric guitar—you name it. The punishment seemed silly if I sent him to a room where he could have more fun than in an arcade, so I'd come up here and unplug everything and hide the cords!"

The lanai was the center of life at the Morton household, a cozy room despite its size where Lucy and Gary would watch TV, read, or occasionally run a film on a huge screen hidden in the cottage-cheese ceiling. One whole wall of the lanai was glass sliding doors that opened onto the patio. The glass was protected by sliding white iron gates that gave the place a prison look when they were shut.

"We had to put them in," Lucy said, "but we put them in too late. The horse was already out of the barn. We were having dinner right here," she continued pointing to the adjoining dining room, "and somebody climbed over the wall, up the trellis into my bedroom, and walked out with two hundred and fifty thousand dollars' worth of jewelry. We didn't hear a thing."

Except for the addition of the iron gates after the burglary, the house was much the same as when Lucy first moved in. She fiercely resisted change, whether it was in the color of her hair or the fabric of a drape. In September of 1988, a downpour in Palm Springs caused extensive damage to the roof of their house, and a flood destroyed the carpet and drapes. While Gary saw it as a chance to do something different, Lucy was adamant about replacing the damaged articles with exact replicas.

Home life was as important to Lucy in her seventies as it was when she was a child. I had read (in more than one article) that she had a very unhappy childhood, as evidenced by the fact that she was chained to a clothesline for punishment. I asked her about it.

"Nothing could be farther from the

truth," she said shaking her head. "I had a wonderful childhood."

Lucy was born to Henry and Desirée "DeDe" Hunt Ball on August 6, 1911, in Celoron, New York. Henry was a telephone lineman. "He made three dollars a day, and that was a lot of dough in those days. Some people were making a dollar a week!"

About a year after Lucy's birth, Henry Ball was asked to go to work for Anaconda Copper in Montana, where he could make five dollars a week. DeDe thought it would be a magnificent adventure. She packed Lucy and Henry's things, and the three of them went off to tame the Wild West. After two years, Henry came down with typhoid fever, and DeDe decided to take him back to Jamestown for better medical treatment and to be near relatives when the child they were expecting was born. They made it as far as Wyandotte, Michigan, when Henry died on February 28, 1915.

Although she was only three, Lucy vividly remembered the day her father died. "I knew something was very wrong, because my mother wouldn't let me see him for a week. He was running a very high fever and he was very contagious. We were quarantined, and so I couldn't go out and play with the other kids, which was all I wanted to do. I was trying to amuse myself with something when a bird flew in the window. It was a big black bird, like a crow, and it flew all around the living room, fluttering its wings and squawking. It got stuck in the transverse of the drapes. I was trying to catch it, just for something to do, and my mother came out and told me that Daddy was gone. As soon as she said it, a painting of a schooner in a violent storm fell off the wall. To this day, when a picture falls off a wall, I think somebody has died."

DeDe, now four months pregnant with Lucy's brother, Fred, took Lucy and the body of her husband back to Celoron, where Henry was buried. Lucy's maternal grandfather, Fred Hunt, became the head of the family, and Lucy always referred to him as Dad. She joked that when she saw the Kaufman and Hart play *You Can't Take It with You*, a comedy about a family of zany individualists, she thought the authors had taken a peek through the Hunt-Ball keyhole.

"I loved to explore. I loved to see what was on the other side of a fence, or over a wall, or the view from a tree. It always got me into some kind of trouble. When I was about six or seven, I used to play for hours with the little boy down the street, and he taught me the best games. My mother didn't agree. I was with him one afternoon, and when I got back, my mother asked me where I was. I told her I was playing with little Jimmy down the street.

"'That's nice, Lucille. What did you play?'

"'I told her we played Milk the Cow! Well, her eyes bugged out like a fly." Lucy did an imitation of her mother in high indignation. "'You played what?'

"'We played Milk the Cow!'

"'Well,' she said, putting her hands on her hips, 'which one of you was the cow?'

"'Jimmy was,' I told her. 'Besides, I couldn't be the cow. I don't have one of those things.' That was the end of Milk the Cow.

"It was my mother who tied a rope around my waist and then attached it to the clothesline. She didn't do it to be mean. She did it because I wandered all over the place. I always wanted to see what was going on down the street or in the town, but it wasn't because I hated home. Not at all. I was curious. I had a wonderful childhood. My stepfather never tied me up. My mother didn't marry him until I was almost ten years old, and by that time you couldn't keep me tied up with iron chains."

Lucy remembered her stepfather, Ed Peterson. "My stepfather was just kind of dull. He drank a lot, but he wasn't abusive. The one thing he did give me was a love of reading. He had a tremendous library (for those days) of books, which he encouraged me to read. My favorite author was Zane Grey. I loved the tales of the Old West, and I used to act them out all the time with my imaginary friends Madeline and Sassafrassa. I used to drive my mother crazy, begging her to buy me a horse. I think one of the reasons I wanted to leave home was that there weren't a lot of kids my age around. I wanted to play with somebody without having to make them up."

Lucy suddenly remembered something that she hadn't thought of in over fifty years. "When I was about twelve or thirteen, I would go to the movies in Jamestown all by myself. The silents. Chaplin. Swanson. Clara Bow. They had a terrific influence on me. My favorite movies were the ones with William S. Hart and Tom Mix and Pearl White. Anyway, the theater was about a mile from our house, and I would walk back and forth. I was never afraid, even though it was pitch-black on the way home." She sat back in her chair and took a deep breath.

"What happened?" I asked.

"Well, one night I was coming home from the movies and walking down the road, when I heard somebody walking behind me. I guess I thought it was an animal or something, until the footsteps started picking up, and I got the feeling that it was somebody trying to catch up with me. I turned around and saw it was a friend of my stepfather's. I knew the guy—not well, but I knew him —and he started to walk alongside of me. I remember he wasn't much older than I was. He started asking me about the picture I had seen, which I thought was a little strange. I mean, how did he know I was at the movies? Well, we walked along a little more, and he put his arm around me. I squirmed away from him and BAM! He threw me down on the ground. I remember I rolled down into some bushes before I was stopped by a solid object. I thought it was a tree until it started to move, and I looked up and saw my step-father. He told the boy to get lost, which he did in a hurry, and we walked home together without ever mentioning the incident. I don't think we *ever* talked about it. The funny thing is that the boy who jumped me just disappeared. He ran away, I guess, but he was sure never seen in town again."

I asked her, "What do you think your stepfather was doing out there? Do you think he knew what the kid was going to do?"

She looked puzzled. "I don't know. It didn't strike me as odd until you just said that. I just know that he was there and broke the fall. Strange, isn't it?"

Lucy was born with a wanderlust. Jamestown is right smack between Chicago and New York City, five hundred miles in either direction. Lucy never gave any thought to Chicago. She always had her sights set on Manhattan. I asked her why.

"I guess they never made any glamorous movies about Chicago. Just the one about the cow that started the fire. In the movies, all the sophisticated people lived in New York, and that's where I wanted to be." After Lucy made several unsuccessful attempts at leaving home, DeDe realized her ambitions couldn't be squelched. ("I wasn't running away from anyplace or anyone. I wanted to be an actress and I had to go to New York to do it.") DeDe finally gave her daughter permission to leave Jamestown to find her fame and fortune. The day she left, Lucy was fifteen years old.

CHAPTER
Four

LUCY HAD A hard time concentrating on our
game one afternoon because she was in too
much pain. She had been having trouble
with her teeth. Gumboils and old caps were
making her wince. She went to see her dentist in Westwood, who told her it would cost
about fifteen thousand dollars to get her
mouth back in shape. Lucy didn't mind
spending the money, but the thought of the
twice-weekly visits made her cry. The dental
work was torture for her. She only had one
laugh during the whole ordeal, and it came
in the elevator on the way to the dentist's
office.

Lucy never made entrances. She kept her
head down as she and Frank got on the elevator, and stepped to the back of the car as
it filled up with other passengers. As the
doors closed, the man next to her whispered
in her ear, "You look like Lucille Ball."

Without uttering a sound, Lucy shook her
head and mouthed, "I am."

With a knee-jerk reaction, the man
screamed at the top of his lungs, "Oh my

God! It's Lucille Ball!" It scared Lucy so much that she almost went straight up through the escape hatch. Lucy looked at the man and said, "You scared me." With that, everyone broke up, and the whole car shook with laughter.

I was waiting for Lucy when she got back from the dentist. Her mouth was numb. She poured us each a glass of lemonade. Up until that day, I had been drinking water or soda in the afternoon, but I thought I'd try the lemonade that Lucy raved about. I took a sip and shuddered. It was like paint thinner on ice. The worst lemonade I ever tasted. Lucy took a big gulp and said, "Mmmmmmmmmm. Good." Then I realized her mouth was shot up with Novocain and was still numb. I didn't want to offend her, so I held my nose and finished it. Ick!

When Gary came home, he presented Lucy with an offer he'd received earlier in the day. The Sony Corporation wanted Lucy to do a commercial that would be seen in Japan only. For one day's work, Sony would pay her $800,000. She turned it down. She mused, "There was a time when I didn't even think that much money existed."

Lucy had fifty dollars sewn into her underwear when she left for New York in 1926 to study acting at the John Murray Anderson–Robert Milton School of Dramatic Art. It was the most prestigious acting school in America, and she had to audition to be admitted.

"I agonized over what I should do for my monologue. I thought Juliet was too high-hat, and besides, everybody did Juliet, so I did one of Julius Tannen's pieces."

Julius Tannen was a famous actor of the Yiddish theater who used to tour the country between his New York engagements. Whenever Tannen played Jamestown, Lucy's stepfather, Ed, who was a great fan of the theater, took Lucy to see his performance. Although Tannen had never achieved "star" status in the mainstream of American theater, a legendary story about the actor was widely circulated. I asked Lucy if she knew the story. She laughed and said she did. She remembered the first time she heard it was when she got to New York, because it was the first time she ever heard a "swear word" come out of the mouth of one of her peers.

"When I told one of the other girls in class I had auditioned with a Tannen piece, she told me the story. I was absolutely aghast, but I sure laughed."

The story went like this. Julius Tannen

was notorious for picking up ladies of the night whenever he finished a show. He was also notorious for being extremely cheap. One night while he was on the road, he picked up a prostitute who had no idea who he was, and they went back to his hotel room. When the two had finished their business, Tannen took his wallet from the bureau, pulled out two pieces of paper, and handed them to the girl.

"What's this?" asked the hooker.

"With my compliments, darling," he said in his most Shakespearean voice, "two tickets for tomorrow night's performance."

The hooker took the tickets, tore them up, and threw the pieces in Tannen's face. "I don't want tickets! I want dough!"

Tannen looked at the girl and said, "Darling, you want dough? Then fuck a baker!"

Although Lucy had enough talent to get her into the school, she was told by Mr. Milton that she was wasting her time. He asked her to watch one of the seniors of the school do a scene and then tell him if she thought she could do as well. Lucy went to the back of the class and watched the girl perform. "God, she was great. Even then. So quirky and original. I wanted to crawl under one of the chairs." The girl was Bette

Davis. (Ironically, Davis herself was earlier rejected for admission to another drama school, run by actress Eva LeGallienne, who had dismissed the young Bette as "a frivolous little girl.")

While Lucy struggled at acting school, she worked as a model for Hattie Carnegie, one of the top fashion designers of the time. "Hattie was a great gal. She really cared for her girls. I used to model for Joan Bennett when she would come into the salon, because we were the same size and Hattie thought we looked alike. We both had pug noses anyway. That's when I changed my name."

"To what?"

"I was Diane Belmont. I always liked the name Diane, and I was going past Belmont Race Track in Queens and I thought a model should have a more sophisticated name than Lucille Ball. It's funny, but when I first got to Hollywood, I ran into one of the girls I used to work with, who ran up to me and said, 'Hello, Diane!' I looked behind me to see who she was talking to, and then I realized it was me. I told her I was no longer Diane Belmont, I was now Lucille Ball. She looked at me and said, 'Why change a wonderful name like Diane Belmont to a lousy name like Lucille Ball? You'd better go back to your real name, honey. You'll do much better.'"

Sometimes when Gary would come in from work, he'd call out, "I'm home, Diane!"

Lucy recalled that she went to Washington with Hattie for a show for the wives of congressmen and senators. While the other girls stayed on to sightsee, Lucy took the train back to New York for a class.

"I was sitting by myself when the train pulled into Baltimore and a very beautiful girl got on, very well dressed, and sat next to me. She pulled out a flask and offered me a drink. I didn't take it, but we started talking, and she asked me what I did. I told her that I was an actress and a model and that I worked at Hattie Carnegie's. She asked me if I had any plans when we got back to town, and I told her I didn't but that I was also very tired from the whirlwind trip to Washington and I didn't want any. When the train pulled into Penn Station, the girl offered me a ride back to my place. I was staying at the Hotel Kimberly at Seventy-fourth and Amsterdam. [A favorite of every young actress trying to break into show business.] I was very impressed that she could afford a cab, and I accepted. The girl told me that she had two friends coming in from out of town, and would I please go out to dinner with them? I wasn't in the habit of going out with strangers, but I also wasn't in the habit of turning down a free meal. After she insisted a few times and told me they were very nice men, I said okay. The girl came back up to my room, and went through my closet and chose the dress I should wear. It was one of my best dresses. She helped me with my hair, gave me a spritz of the perfume, and it's like we're two old girlfriends playing dress-up. So off we went.

"When we got to the restaurant, I was surprised, because it seemed more like a bar and grill, and I felt very overdressed. The place was almost empty except for two men who were at the bar who never took their eyes off of us as we crossed the room. They looked like a couple of thugs. I started to feel very uncomfortable, and got really scared when the girl left the table and one of the men got off of the bar stool and walked over to me. Gee, I must have been all of sixteen or seventeen at the time, but I knew what the man wanted . . . or at least I thought I did. You didn't have to be down on the farm to play Milk the Cow! He asked me to come with him, and I said no. He asked me how well I knew my 'friend,' and I told him I had met her that day on the train. Now, I was about on the verge of tears. He asked me again to go with him, and when I said no again, he pulled out a badge and showed me he was a cop.

"I went outside with him, and he told me that the girl I was with was one of the foremost call girls in New York. He referred to her as a 'hundred-dollar-a-night girl.' Now, I *did* break down. With all the makeup she put on me, this guy thinks I'm a hooker, too. I started bawling all over the place, and I told him that I wasn't a hundred-dollar-a-night girl. I was an actress. He laughed, put his arm around me, and told me to get into the unmarked police car. I was crying, 'Please don't take me to jail; all I wanted was my dinner.'

"No," he said, "I'm going to take you home." He did. He told me I was a good girl and wished me luck. God, was I naive."

The girls at the Kimberly Hotel took Lucy under their wing, and whenever they had a boyfriend with a friend who needed a date, they would turn to Lucy. "They all knew I was going out for dinner and nothing else, but we still had a racket going.

"I remember the first time I went to '21.'

One of the girls asked me to double-date, and trained me thoroughly before we left. These were the rules. First, I had to bring the biggest purse I had and line it with wax paper. Here I was, dressed for the evening, carrying a satchel with me. Then, whenever we went to the ladies' room, we would ask our date for a quarter to give to the attendant, which we would then pocket. She showed me how to swipe a roll from the table when the boys weren't looking, scoop out the center part, and put it in my purse to wait for the meat course. Then we'd make sandwiches under the table right in the big purses we'd brought. That's why we lined them with wax paper. We were making our lunches for the next week. I think that night we went to the bathroom half a dozen times. The poor guys thought we had diarrhea or severe kidney problems. Up and down, up and down, all night. They were gentlemen, so when we got up, they would get up. The four of us up and down all night like carousel horses. The poor slobs didn't even get a goodnight kiss."

We took a break from our backgammon game, and I asked Lucy to do me a favor and call my friend Dick Bell, an actor, as a surprise for his birthday. I dialed his number in New York, and when he answered, the first voice he heard was Lucy's, singing "Happy Birthday" in a low, grumbling tone that resembled the rolling sound of an oncoming earthquake. Dick, a mega-Lucy freak, was flabbergasted. His first reaction was to ask if it was me doing an imitation of Lucy. I was on the extension, and assured him he had the one and only Lucille Ball on the other end.

"I love you, Lucy!" he blurted out.

"Thank you!" she said, and asked him some questions about where he was and what he was up to. He told her that he used to live across the street from the Hotel Kimberly at Seventy-fourth and Amsterdam.

"Do you remember it?" he asked.

Lucy roared, "Do I remember it? How could I forget it? I had a lot of fun in that place. It was like a sorority. That's where I got shot at."

"Shot at?" he asked.

"Yeah. I was sitting in the bathtub taking a soak, when a bullet came through the window and went right between my legs."

Dick asked her, "Where were your legs?"

I could see her reaction to the question. She didn't understand that he meant "How were your legs positioned?"

She answered him, "Where were my legs? They were in the tub with the rest of me!"

"Was somebody shooting at you?"

"No. There was a speakeasy across the street, and there was always some kind of trouble going on at that corner. They were shooting at somebody downstairs, and the bullet ricocheted off a streetlamp and right into my bathtub. Jesus! There was water everywhere. I never thought I'd get killed taking a bath."

Lucy had a parting of the ways with the Anderson/Milton School of Dramatic Art, but knew that she wasn't ready to go back to Jamestown. "I couldn't be a failure at seventeen."

She stayed on at Hattie Carnegie's as a model until tragedy struck.

"I was working one afternoon; it was just after lunch, and there was a big show. The salon was packed. Everybody was there, including Joan Bennett, and I made my first entrance. I got right to the middle of the floor, and all of a sudden it was like two hot pokers were stuck through my feet and right up my legs. Well, down I went. Right in front of everybody. God, I've never felt pain like that in my life. All these high-class dames just looked at me as if I were crazy

. . . lying on the floor screaming and writhing. Hattie came over and picked me up. God, she was a great lady. She let the show go on, but she took me in a cab to see her doctor. I screamed all the way. He told me it was rheumatoid arthritis, and that I was going to have to spend the next few months in bed."

Lucy was devastated. She wanted to stay in New York, but she had no money and there was no one to take care of her. Hattie Carnegie paid for her medical bills and her transportation back to Jamestown.

The doctor was wrong about one thing. Lucy would not have to spend the next few months in bed—it would be the next few *years*.

"I know it's a terrible thing to say, but I think my mother was secretly happy that I was crippled. At least it kept me at home. My one regret was that I never finished high school, but I read to make up for it. I learned more in those two years than I ever did in school. Especially that if you don't have your health, nothing else matters. I read everything I could get my hands on. History, biography, novels. I reread everything that Zane Grey wrote three times. I must have read every book in the Jamestown library."

Even though she had residual pain, as soon as Lucy could walk again, she headed right back for the railroad station and New York. "I stayed with one of the other models over near Tudor City on Forty-second Street. The first day back in New York was the coldest day I had ever experienced in my life. I had about four layers of clothes on, and they still didn't keep out the chill. As I walked down the street, my legs still killing me, I looked up to see right there in front of me one of the most famous movie stars in the world. Coming right at me. I went crazy. I had to meet her. I had to shake her hand. I went up to her and got right into her face before she knew what was happening. I took her hand, squeezed it and screamed, 'ZaSu Pitts!' The *P* in Pitts exploded in a spray of saliva in the poor woman's face, and it was so cold that it froze into an ice mask before she knew what hit her. She looked at me as if I had just escaped from Bellevue (as well she should have), because it wasn't ZaSu Pitts. It was Lillian Gish! I met her at a Hollywood party about twenty years later, and asked her if she remembered the incident. She did! I guess you'd remember anybody who'd spit in your face and called you ZaSu!"

Hattie Carnegie was as good as her word, and Lucy was given her job back. Hattie taught Lucy how to dress, how to stand, and how to walk with grace again. She never forgot it. Gary would often say that "whenever Lucy entered a room, the way she stood, the way she held her carriage, you knew a thoroughbred had just come out of the gate."

Lucy bleached her hair blond and picked up a few modeling assignments, including a stint as the Chesterfield poster girl. She auditioned for some Broadway shows, but got rejected at every turn.

"I couldn't sing. I couldn't dance. I didn't know how to act. I sat in front of a camera and smiled, and that was it. Nobody told me you needed talent to be an actress!"

Lucy was making the rounds of the managers' offices one day when she ran into a friend in front of the Palace Theatre. The friend told her that Samuel Goldwyn Studios was in town looking for poster girls to appear in the upcoming Eddie Cantor feature *Roman Scandals*—a Hollywood movie contract! The Goldwyn people had all the girls chosen until one had to drop out because her mother would rather see her in hell than in Hollywood. They were desperate for a replacement; the train was leaving the next day.

Lucy got the man's name, told him about her Chesterfield poster, and he offered her the job. Lucy was in the right place at the right time. Did she want to be a Goldwyn Girl?

Lucy couldn't give an answer right away, but told the friend she'd call the next day with her decision. She went right to her surrogate mother, Hattie Carnegie, who told her, "Child, when opportunity knocks, open the door." Lucy did. In the summer of 1932, she traded the extremely hot streets of New York for the unbelievably hot desert of California.

CHAPTER
Five

LUCIE ARNAZ DROPPED by to see her mother one afternoon while we were in midgame. She came by often when she was in the neighborhood. They kissed, and Lucy said to her daughter, "You're too thin. Have you got anorexia?"

"No," said Lucie. "I have a husband, five children, a career, and no time to eat."

We had been listening to an Andrews Sisters record just before Lucie arrived, which reminded her mother of one of her favorite *Here's Lucy* shows. It featured Patti Andrews. In a big musical finale, Lucy played Maxene; Lucie, LaVerne; and Patti, herself, singing "Boogie Woogie Bugle Boy from Company B."

Lucille wanted to watch it, and the three of us went to the den. Gary was sitting in his easy chair, about to get displaced. I felt like Larry from *The Bob Newhart Show* as I walked in with the two girls. I said to Gary, "Hello, I'm Jim. This is my friend Lucy, and this is my other friend Lucie."

Lucille collected favorite moments from different shows on one reel. Most of them were big production numbers, including a hoe-down, (where Lucie exits the wrong way and dances right into a piece of scenery) and a Hawaiian number doing the hula in grass skirts. Lucille wrinkled her nose and said, "We wanted to do that whole show in Hawaii, but the network said it was too expensive."

After watching for about a half hour, Lucie told us that she had just turned down a movie-of-the-week.

"Why the hell did you turn it down?" asked her mother.

"Why? Because they wanted to give me

second billing behind Shelley Hack." Her mother shook her head.

Lucie left a few minutes later, and it was hard for her mother to contain her disapproval. "She wouldn't take second billing to Shelley Hack. What the hell difference does it make where she was billed? She would have been acting. If you're an actress, you have to act, no matter the part, no matter if you're getting paid or not. Billing! You work all your life to get your name up in lights, and then a hundred-dollar-a-week janitor comes along and blows a fuse and then where are you?"

That was advice straight from the mouth of the "Queen of the B's." "I never cared whether I was A pictures, B pictures, C, D, or F ones. As long as I was working."

Unlike a lot of aspiring actresses, Lucy came to Hollywood with a job in hand. She was a "Goldwyn Girl," making over a hundred dollars a week. In *Roman Scandals*, she was one of several slave girls who were chained to a wall, nude to the waist, covered only with volumes of curls cascading from a blond wig. "I still have the G-string!" One of many girls, she stepped out of the chorus when she volunteered to take a pie in the face.

She followed *Roman Scandals* with a bit part in *Kid Millions,* another Eddie Cantor opus, where Lucy first met and made a life-long friend of Ethel Merman. "Merman was a great gal . . . really down-to-earth. No bullshit. But she always fell in love with the wrong guy for her."

Merman was married four times, her last marriage to Ernie Borgnine being the shortest (six weeks) and the most famous. "I gave the Merm her shower when she married Ernie. The party lasted almost as long as the marriage. She and Ernie went off to Japan for their honeymoon, and were back the next day. Merman showed up on my doorstep," Lucy told me. "I said, 'What happened?' and she said, 'Don't ask!' She was in my guest house for a week before she went back to New York. Every time I went by, all I could hear was her crying. You always thought of her as such a tough dame, but she was really a pushover for a guy. They went at it like Dempsey and Tunney."

Lucy was disenchanted with being a Goldwyn Girl. She wanted speaking parts, but all Mr. Goldwyn would do was let her look pretty and smile. She had friends over at Columbia who told her it was fun on their lot. They did all the comedies. Lucy always knew that she could do comedy, and wanted the chance to try it.

One of her first assignments at Columbia was with the Three Stooges in *Three Little Pigskins* in 1934. I asked her what she learned from the outrageous masters of slapstick.

"I learned that seltzer up your nose really hurts!"

Lucy was frustrated at Columbia, because they put her in heavy dramas. But she felt she was always learning something, and made the most of it.

I remembered one of our Sherwood Oaks classes. A disgustingly perky blonde asked Lucy, "What can I do to become a star?"

Lucy harrumphed, "That's the stupidest question I ever heard." The girl shrank back into her seat. Lucy continued, "Don't ask me what to do to be a star. Ask me how you can learn. And the answer to that is do everything you can to be in the business. Around the business. Meet people in the business, and do what they tell you to do."

She told us that the only real goal she had when she came to Hollywood was to be a part of the movie business. She felt she got to Hollywood by an extraordinary piece of good luck, and the only thing she had to offer when she got there was her energy. She was working, and she was learning.

She said, "I tried to do what they asked me to do, and sometimes I got that little feeling in the pit of my tummy that I had learned something. And I was so happy when I felt I had learned something."

"I think that might have been the worst time in my life. God, I was lonely." She was renting a dismal studio apartment in Hollywood to save enough money to bring her mother out. For a town that's known for glamour, some parts of Hollywood are the seediest places in the world.

When she had enough money, she called her mother, who was now divorced from Ed Peterson. Lucy asked her mother to come live with her. DeDe told her that she'd love to but couldn't just leave Grandpa Hunt and Lucy's brother, Fred. Lucy said she had enough to support them all and told the whole family to come westward-ho.

The first night her family was in town, Lucille borrowed a friend's convertible and took her mother for a tour. At midnight, they drove to the top of Mulholland Drive, famous for its panoramic vistas of the Los Angeles basin on one side and the San Fernando Valley on the other, and also as one of the most notorious necking spots in America.

Lucy found a place to park, and DeDe was overwhelmed not only by the beauty of the scene but by seeing her daughter after such a long absence. "My mother started to cry, and I put my arm around her. We sat there silently for a few minutes, when all of a sudden there was a cop next to us. He banged his nightstick against the running board and said, 'Okay, you dames. None of that stuff up here. We don't go for that shit here. Run along, butch.'" Lucy shook her head and laughed. "Can you imagine? He thought we were lesbians."

Lucy said, "I don't think my mother had ever heard the word 'lesbian,' and when I told her what it meant and that the cop thought we were necking, she cried all the way home."

Minutes after the family arrived, Lucy got a job in *Roberta* with Fred Astaire and Ginger Rogers. She walked down a staircase in a fashion show wearing a white satin dress and white ostrich-feather cape. Lucy told me that she did it exactly the way Hattie Carnegie had taught her to walk and turn. She stood out in the sequence and was offered a seven-year contract by the young RKO studio chief, Pandro Berman.

Lucy told me, "I was taking my morning walk not long ago. Gary and I would sometimes take the car over to Rodeo Drive and then walk around and look in the store windows. This old man shuffled by me and said, 'Hello, Lucille!' and I said hello back and kept on going. I said to Gary that he looked kind of familiar, and Gary said, 'That was Pan Berman!' Jesus! And I used to date him."

Getting a contract with a major studio made Lucy feel she was going to college at last. The RKO lot was her campus, and the other contract players were her fraternity brothers and sisters. The stars and directors were her teachers.

"Contract players were just that. You were under contract to do whatever picture the studio wanted to put you in, and in whatever capacity. They could make you stand around, or they could give you lines. If you were physically right for it, they made you do it. If they wanted a dance-hall hostess, you were a dance-hall hostess. If they wanted a nun, you were a nun. It was all I could wish for. We had to be available for publicity pictures, and you learned how to conduct yourself on a set and not make any noise. It was being around the studio that was so great. You'd meet stars. You'd meet directors and producers, and they'd remember you and give you lines and bits and things. But it was always what I wanted. I was in the 'biz,' and I had a contract. I was making money at what I loved to do."

"Did you ever object to anything?"

"The only thing I objected to was the heat in the [San Fernando] Valley. I never made demands. I knew that I could go far if I paid attention and was liked—they didn't like troublemakers. . . . I was learning and being paid for it."

Lucy was learning under the tutelage of one of the great stage mothers of all time, Lela Rogers. Lela had guided her daughter, Ginger, to stardom, and RKO put Lela under contract to develop the talents of other young performers. They gave Lela the Little Theatre on the RKO lot, where she would produce and direct plays that featured the contract players.

Lucy remembered Lela fondly. "It was a wonderful thing. Besides taking care of Ginger, she would take classes with some of the great drama coaches of the time and then race back to our little workshop and share with us what she had just learned herself. We took classes three or four times a week. Lela was very helpful in making my career what it was."

When Lucy signed her contract, the studio had to compose an official biography of the young player.

"I thought saying I was from Jamestown was just too dull. I love Jamestown now, but then, it was like coming from East Japip. So I told them I came from Butte, Montana, which was somewhat true, since I was there for a year when I was a little girl. Well, the studio loved that. All of a sudden, I was 'Two-Gun Lu!' I wrote to the Butte Chamber of Commerce and told them to send me everything there was to know about the place. I knew all the streets, I knew all the shops that were there, I knew all the important people in the town. I knew more about Butte than the 'Butties' did! I could talk fluently about it, even though I hadn't been there since I was three."

"It was Lela who told me that I should try the stage. She was also the first person who told me I was funny. I had a few lines in a movie called *I Dream Too Much*, starring Henry Fonda. Lela said that one of them put her away."

The scene was Lucy and her family taking a tour of museums. Her character was getting tired, but the tour guide insisted she press on, proclaiming that "this is culture."

"I don't want any more culture," said Lucille. "It makes my feet hurt."

Lucy loved working in that little playhouse. There was something about a live audience that always got her. It reminded her of when she was in high school and doing the school plays. Applause was like a shot of adrenaline to her.

One of Lucy's not-so-secret ambitions was to be a Broadway star. It was a way to show Mr. Anderson and Mr. Milton of the drama school that they were wrong about her. She thought she had her chance in late 1936 when she was signed to play the ingenue lead in the comedy *Hey Diddle Diddle*, starring silent-film idol Conway Tearle.

Although Lucy got good notices in an undistinguished role, the show never made it to Broadway. Conway Tearle died, and Lucy returned to California. She would have to wait almost twenty-five years before she set foot on a Broadway stage.

RKO had acquired the screen rights to Edna Ferber and George S. Kaufman's Broadway hit *Stage Door*, to star Ginger Rogers and Katharine Hepburn. Lela Rogers persuaded Pan Berman and director Gregory La Cava to cast Lucille as Judy Canfield. Lela had replaced Hattie as Lucy's guide and mentor.

RKO was taking a chance on La Cava, who was a recovering alcoholic, and the studio began shooting without a finished script. La Cava encouraged the girls to make up the movie as they went along. Lucy wasn't good at improvisation. "I came to him one day terrified because there was only half a scene. I asked him where the rest of the pages were, and he said they didn't have any more pages. I asked him what I should do, and he said 'Make it up!'"

Through Lucy's efforts, Ann Miller was also cast in the picture. Lucy had discovered Ann performing in a night club in San Francisco. "Boy, could that girl dance. She still can." Miller was a mature, sophisticated hoofer, who had been wowing them all over the Bay area. At the time, she was thirteen. Ann had just turned fourteen when *Stage Door* started shooting. "Her mother lied about her age"—Lucy winked—"and I swore to it."

Lucy remembered Hepburn on the set: "She was so beautiful and s-o-o-o slim and s-o-o-o chic and she put me in an absolute panic. Just the way she talked terrified me. [Lucy went into an imitation of Hepburn, pulling down the edges of her lower lip and e-lon-gat-ing each vowel.] She was s-o-o-o highbrow that I never really knew exactly what she was saying, but I'd nod my head and agree with her. She never talked to anyone directly, she'd address you looking all around you but never at you. I was riveted to her whenever she was around. She wasn't really standoffish. She ignored everyone equally."

I asked Lucy if they stayed in touch after the picture, and she laughed. "No. But I did hear from her just after my granddaughter was born. What's that . . . almost fifty years later? It was in the paper that Lucie named the child Katharine after Miss Hepburn. Gary and I were sitting here one night, and the phone rang. Gary answered it, and she said, 'Mr. Morton? Is Lucille there? This is Kate Hepburn.' It was one of the few times I saw Gary flustered. He handed me the phone like it was a hot potato and said, 'It's for you.' Kate asked me if it was true that the child had been named after her, and I said she had. After a pause, Hepburn said to me, 'Kath-ar-ine Luck-in-bill! What a long name.' And that was it!"

After her freshman year at RKO, Lucy was promoted from bit parts to speaking parts to featured player. Lucy was assigned first billing after the Marx Brothers in the film version of the Broadway hit *Room Service*. *Room Service* was not one of the brothers' plays. In most of their other movies, they would play Broadway and tour it before going before the cameras. The result was that they had the "business" down pat, and were in tune like a fine machine. They had no such opportunity with *Room Service*, the result being less than what the audience expected from the zany trio. Lucy thought working with the Marx Brothers was like working in the eye of a hurricane. "They really didn't include you in things. It all happened around you, and you reacted to it."

Frank Albertson played the part of Leo Davis, the young playwright who's taken advantage of by the producer (Groucho) and the director (Chico). Lucy and Frank got to be friends. Shortly after the picture wrapped, Frank had to go into the hospital for a hemorrhoid operation. In the late thirties, before the advent of laser surgery, a hemorrhoid operation was a serious and excruciatingly painful procedure.

Lucy and a few of the other contract players went to visit Albertson in the hospital. The nurse was reluctant to let all of them in at one time, but Lucille persuaded her to accommodate them, telling her they were on a lunch break and had to get back before the afternoon shoot. She promised they would be very quiet and respectful of Frank's delicate condition. Lucy was trying to keep from laughing as she said, "When we walked into Frank's room, he was lying on the bed moaning in agony. The poor guy was really suffering. He knew we were up to no good the minute he saw us, and begged us to leave. Well, brother, that's all we needed. We did everything we could to break him up. He shut his eyes as tightly as he could, trying to pretend we weren't there, but it didn't work. He bit his lip so hard it turned purple. He finally gave in, alternating screams of laughter with screams of pain. The nurse came running in like a sketch nurse in a vaudeville scene, and threw us all out on the spot. As I was leaving, Frank looked at me with the purplest face I've ever seen, and said, 'I never knew that my eyelids were connected to my asshole.'"

Lucy was well liked around the studio, and she graduated to leading roles in small pictures. "Eventually, they started sending me scripts and asked me if I'd like to do this or that. It was a big thrill. One day I saw a casting sheet that said 'A Lucille Ball type,' and that was the biggest thrill I ever had. I went into the casting office and told them I'd be available in a week, and they told me I was wrong for the part. Imagine!"

CHAPTER
Six

"IT'S AN EGO trip!" Lucy declared. Gary had just bought a new Bentley for about $100,000. "What do we need another car for?" Lucy had a gold Mercedes that Frank drove her around in, and the staff had cars provided by her. Gary already had a Rolls-Royce and two other cars, and she couldn't understand why he needed the Bentley. "Oh, well," she said, resigned to it, "at least he doesn't drink or carouse. If he wants the car, he can afford it."

I asked Lucy if she remembered her yellow convertible. She was surprised. She remembered it very well, but wondered how

I knew about it. I told her that I read a couple of different accounts of how her grandfather's fight with the city of Los Angeles almost destroyed her first classy car. She said it was true.

When the city wouldn't remove a tree from in front of the Ogden Drive house, Fred cut away at its roots each day, hoping it would fall over. Then the city would *have* to remove it. He got his wish when the tree fell over during a rainstorm, a few minutes after Lucille parked her brand-new yellow convertible right under it. "It cost almost as much to have fixed as it did to buy. Dad wanted us to sue the city for negligence," she said. "My grandfather was always getting us into some jam."

Lucy had been going through her scrapbooks. Every day for a few weeks, Tom Watson, publicist for Lucille Ball Productions, worked on them. There were at least ten, and maybe twenty of the huge books. When Tom finished one, cutting and repasting all the yellowed clippings and photos, he would put it in the formal living room on a stack on the floor.

Lucy got up and told me to come into the living room with her. She got down on her hands and knees, found the scrapbook she was looking for, sat cross-legged on the carpet, and opened it. She pointed to a small black-and-white photo of an old man sitting on a chair on a porch. "This is my grandfather," Lucy said, "but he was more like my father."

By today's standards, Fred Hunt would be known as "the nutty old man down the block." In fact, even in the thirties, he was known as "the nutty old man down the block." Lucy said, "He was thrown off every street corner in Hollywood. He used to go down to Sunset and give speeches about Eugene Debs for president. When Roosevelt was running for reelection in 1936, Dad gave speech after speech about Debs being the only man to pull the country out of the Depression. People thought he was nuts, because one, he screamed at them, two, we were already coming out of the Depression, and three, Debs died in 1926."

When Fred got too old to stand on street corners, he would take his chair off the front porch and put it in the middle of the street to yell at the cars as they drove by. Lucy came home one afternoon with Hal King and found her grandfather sitting on his chair in the middle of the sidewalk preaching to anyone within earshot. Lucy and Hal tried to talk him into going back inside, but he wouldn't budge.

Grandpa joined all the socialist organizations in Hollywood, signed up the rest of the family without their permission, and offered the Ogden Drive house for meetings. When DeDe or Lucy or Fred objected, Dad would go into one of his tantrum fits and turn red in the face until they thought he was having a stroke. When he asked his family to register as Communists, they did so only to keep him quiet.

Lucy looked at the picture and said, "He was off, all right. Today, they would have given him something. Some medication. We just didn't know about such things back then." Lucy and her brother, Fred, suffered repeated embarrassments at home when one of their dates expressed a political viewpoint different from Dad's. Lucy decided, rather than come home to constant questioning and harassment, to keep her mailing address at Ogden Drive but move into a small apartment of her own.

Lucy was well known around town as a "regular girl." She was always on time for work, and she was always smiling. She took direction, and almost never offered her own ideas. She was living out her childhood fantasy. She had fun making movies but hated auditioning. She was loose in front of a camera or an audience but tight and unnatural in a conference room with one producer sitting in judgment; until one audition changed her fear forever.

Lucille, along with every other actress in Hollywood, was asked to audition for the role of Scarlett O'Hara in *Gone With the Wind*. "I thought I'd be more suited for Mammy than I was for Scarlett, but when Mr. Selznick wanted you to read, you read. I thought I should make the most out of it, and so I went out and bought a whole new outfit—real southern—chiffon dress and big picture hat in a matching flower print. I got in the famous yellow convertible, which still had big dents across the back doors, and decided to go through the gates of Selznick's studio in Culver City looking like a star. Well, that morning the radio said we'd have high clouds all day—overcast, but definitely no rain. As soon as I stepped into the car, those high clouds got pretty low in a very big hurry. The skies opened up. The most unbelievable downpour you ever saw—and it just kept coming in buckets and buckets. I can't get the top up because of where the tree hit it. I don't know where the hell Culver City is. I can't find Culver City to this day.

"When I got to the gates of the studio, the car looked like a swimming pool on wheels. I opened the door to get out, and the flood almost knocked two people over. It let loose a torrent that looked like white water gushing over rocks. I made my way up to his office like a drowned rat. Everything was soaked. The hat was drooping around my head, the dress was ruined. The secretary looked at me when I walked in and gasped. I'll never forget what she said . . . 'Is it raining out?' " Lucy repeated the phrase with disgust.

She continued, "There was a fire going in Selznick's office, and since he was going to be late, she told me to go in and sit by the fire to dry. She took a decanter of brandy off his desk and offered me a glass. I was shaking so much and so chilled that I took it and downed it in one gulp. She offered me another, and I downed that, too. By the time Selznick came in, I was smashed. He asked me to do the scene I had prepared, which I did. I was reading Scarlett's speech to Ashley, the one where they don't see Rhett on the sofa, looking like I went over Niagara Falls in a barrel. Selznick was very polite, but even in my stupor I could tell it wasn't going over very well. After I finished, he told me that it was interesting and that I was very brave to make such a choice. I didn't know what he was talking about. He said, 'To do the scene on your knees like that!' I was on my knees the whole time, and never even knew it!"

Lucy was home one night listening to the radio. She was tuned in to a program featuring unemployed people who came on to talk about themselves, hoping that some needy boss might call in with a job. As Lucy listened, she heard the voice of Harriet. Harriet was twenty-seven (Lucy's age), and said that she wanted to be a lady's maid. Her qualifications were that she was honest, loyal, and a tireless worker. She had been taught well by her mother, who was personal maid to Mary Livingston, wife of Jack Benny. Although she was supporting herself and her family, Lucy thought she had enough money left over for one more, so she called the station and hired Harriet.

Because they were the same age, Lucy said that they were more like sisters than employer/employee. Grandpa Hunt, thinking like a good socialist, reprimanded Lucy for hiring a maid. He told her that it perpetuated the struggle of the classes. Lucy countered that she was providing employment. Sometimes they would have these discussions about whether or not Harriet was being exploited in front of Harriet, who sat and listened with great interest.

Lucy told a funny story that *wasn't* funny to Harriet at the time. Lucy misplaced a quilt that her mother had made and was getting frustrated that she couldn't find it. It wasn't at the house or her apartment. The only thing she could imagine was that she left it somewhere at the studio. She looked everywhere before she stormed through the soundstage screaming, "Where's my goddamned afghan? Has anybody seen my damned afghan?" Harriet thought that Lucy was saying "goddamned African," and took offense. She didn't speak to Lucy for a few days, and then offered her resignation. Lucy was dumbstruck at first but, after questioning Harriet, found out what all the fuss was about. Lucy and Harriet remained close until Harriet's death in 1984. "She wasn't my maid," Lucy told me. "She was my friend."

It was in the late thirties that Lucy gained her reputation as "Queen of the B's." Her name was above the title in below-average films that included *The Affairs of Annabel* with Jack Oakie, and its less successful sequel, *Annabel Takes a Tour*; *The Next Time I Marry*; *Panama Lady*; *Twelve Crowded Hours*, with Richard Dix; and *That's Right, You're Wrong*, which featured Kay Kyser and his radio "Kollege of Musical Knowledge."

Lucy was happy with her movie career because it was active, but she wanted her love life to be equally as active. She dated many men, actively seeking a permanent companion and potential papa, but no one was "it" for her. One of the men she was romantically linked with was Cesar Romero. "Cesar's a great guy. I had a real crush on him, and he was terrific fun on a date. The best dancer in the world. One night we went to Mocambo, and we both had too much to drink. I thought that maybe he'd make a pass after all the times we went out, but he didn't. He's a real gent. The best. As we danced, he started to cry. I asked him what was the matter, and he just said, 'I'm strange.' I told him that we were all a little strange, and then he really broke down."

She said Cesar wasn't half as strange as Oscar Levant, whom she dated *once*. Levant was a great friend of George Gershwin, and was in Hollywood to compose movie scores.

His big hit song was "Blame It on My Youth." Aside from writing, Levant started appearing in films, the most notable being *An American in Paris*, in which he played a brooding musical genius much like himself.

In the latter part of his life, Levant was in and out of mental hospitals, receiving shock treatment and wagon-loads of drugs for his manic-depression.

Lucy was apprehensive about her date with Levant (who eventually became her neighbor on Roxbury Drive) but decided to go and have a good time. "He took me up to the top of Mulholland Drive. I kept thinking that if that cop came back, at least I was with a man this time. Oscar parked the car, but just sat there behind the wheel looking out at the lights. He smoked incessantly, and he never said a word. He never even looked at me. Finally, after about a half hour, he looked up at me with these big puppy-dog eyes and took my hand and said, 'Well, I guess you're wondering why I haven't made a pass at you.'

"I just looked at him. I didn't know what to say. If I said yes, I thought he'd kiss me and I'd scream, and if I said no, I thought he'd do it anyway and I'd scream. Then he said, 'Well, don't worry. I'm not going to make a pass at you. I have syphilis.' I don't know if he was kidding or not, but that was the end of it. He started the car and took me home without saying another word." (According to Oscar's widow, June Levant, he *was* kidding.)

Lucy also dated Hal King at the time. "One day Hal and I were at the Santa Monica pier, and there was a fortune-teller. We decided to go in and have our palms read. Hal picks up the story: 'The Gypsy looked at my palm and told me I was from a large family, and that although I loved the girl I was with [Lucy], I would never marry her. Then she looked at Lucy's palm and said one thing I'll never forget. She said, 'Young lady, one day you will be the richest woman and the biggest star in Hollywood.' Lucy took it with a grain of salt. She said, 'The Gypsy told every young girl who looked like an actress the same thing, because that's what they wanted to hear.'" If that's so, the Gypsy was correct at least once in her life.

The most serious of Lucille's romances at that time was a director named Alexander Hall. "He was a nice man," Lucy said, "but he was just dull."

She talked about the fact that she loved to gamble. In the late thirties and early forties, gala gambling boats would sail past the three-mile limit, and people would gamble for the weekend. Lucy and Al Hall took many junkets together, one of which she remembered vividly. "One night we took one of those gambling ships out when gambling was fun."

I interrupted her. "You mean it isn't fun anymore?"

She shook her head. "Not the way I've been taken. Vegas is all right, but Puerto Rico and parts of Europe, they cheated me out of thousands of dollars. Very dishonest.

"Anyway, Al and I were on the ship and I was shooting craps, and I threw eleven sevens in a row. There was such a crowd around that table yelling and screaming that I could hardly breathe. I wanted to pass the dice and I started to put them down, and this Mafia guy"—as she said this she put one finger on her nose, pushing it to the left—"who I didn't know put a thousand dollars on me and said, 'Roll again.' Well, I rolled again, and it came up seven. The twelfth time in a row. I went right to the bar and drank forty-two—that's right, forty-two—brandies in a row. I had the bartender line them up. I went upstairs to one of the open decks to get some air, and passed out on a deck chair.

"The next day the sun came up and I'm still passed out and nobody knows where I am and I don't wake up until noon with third-degree sunburns all over my body. God, I was on fire."

Lucy started work on a new movie in late 1939. It was called *Dance, Girl, Dance*, and in it she would play a stripper. She was crazy about the part, and found it great fun to be playing a floozy. In one scene, Lucy and costar Maureen O'Hara had a cat fight in which Lucy's character gets a black eye. On the day the fight scene was shot, Lucy and O'Hara went to the commissary for lunch, still in costume and makeup. Although they were both unhurt, they looked tattered, torn, and bruised.

As they walked in, the cast of Lucy's next picture, *Too Many Girls*, was having lunch. George Abbott, the director, spotted Lucy, and waved her over to the table to meet the gang. One of the actors couldn't believe that the black-eyed tramp in front of him was going to play the virginal coed. The director saw the look on the young man's face and brought Lucy down to the end of the table to introduce them. "Lucille Ball," said Mr. Abbott, "I'd like you to meet Desi Arnaz."

CHAPTER
Seven

IN THE LAST year of her life, Lucy had lots of trouble sleeping. She would wake up at five o'clock in the morning and lie in bed with her eyes wide open. The lack of sleep was draining her. She would pick Tinker up from the child's crib next to their king-size bed and bring the dog downstairs to keep her company.

Before dawn, Lucy and the dog would walk around in the backyard, picking at plants, killing time until the rest of the world woke up. They'd go into the kitchen; Lucy would give Tinker her breakfast and make a cup of coffee for herself. Then they'd go into the den, where Lucy would sit in the big chair with Tinker in her lap and read until Gary got up a couple of hours later.

Lucy looked particularly bleary-eyed one day when she said to me, "I almost called you at four-thirty this morning."

"Why didn't you?" I asked her.

"Because if you called me at four-thirty

in the morning, I'd kill you. God, I wish I could sleep. I keep having this dream."

I asked her to tell me the dream. She was eager to talk about it. She'd been having the dream for the last two or three years. It starts at the ocean, where Lucy is sunbathing. As she looks out into the ocean, she sees a horse swimming like a fish to the shore. A man with no face sits on the horse. "He frightened me. He was beautifully dressed, but he had no face, and I just wanted to kill him. I was so angry at him that I beat him up. I pull him off the horse and onto the shore and kick him and hit him, but I can't see his face, so I don't know if I'm hurting him. And I know I want to hurt him. Then I wake up." With a sigh, she added, "Then I *stay* up."

Playing amateur analyst, I told her I thought there was a lot of anger in her dream. She agreed. I asked her who she thought the man was. She swore she had absolutely no idea. She couldn't think of anyone she felt that kind of anger toward or wanted to hurt that much. I told her the images of the sea and horses reminded me of Del Mar, where Desi lived. She leaned forward. "You think it's Desi?"

"Yes."

94

She locked those piercing blue eyes on mine and bored in. After a moment, she blinked and said, "I think you're right." Whatever the relationship was between Lucille Ball and Desi Arnaz, it was intense.

Desiderio Alberto Arnaz y de Acha III was born on March 2, 1917, making him six years younger than Lucille. His father was mayor of Santiago de Cuba and a leader in the Cuban House of Representatives. They were wealthy aristocrats, and Desi, as the only child, was sole beneficiary of all the attention, affection, and family fortune.

Desi was a born entertainer. He loved to sing, picked up the guitar quickly, and had dancing feet. When family parties got dull, Desi would start the conga line. He'd beat his drum and lead all the guests dancing and kicking through the streets of Santiago—his mother holding on to Desi, his father holding on to her, and the aunts, uncles, and cousins holding on to each other. Strangers would tag on to the end of the line, which always wound up back at the house with a hundred more guests than it started with. Once Desi had a big enough audience, he sang to them all night.

The parties stopped abruptly in the summer of 1933, when antigovernment guerrillas burned the Arnaz house to the ground. The family fled to Key West with little more than the clothes on their backs. They went from living in a grand hacienda to a warehouse in Miami Beach where Desi helped his father kill rats before they retired for the night.

In four years, Desi went from singing with his high school band to owning his own nightclub in Miami. A job with Xavier Cugat gave him the name recognition he needed for the backing. Desi formed his own band and opened the new club in Miami, but it didn't do well. Few people were coming, and those who did found nothing special.

One unusually crowded Saturday night, Desi felt he was losing the audience during the show and remembered the dance he used to do at parties. He grabbed his drum, and the room erupted in a conga. Within weeks, Desi's place was the hottest in Miami. Everybody wanted to conga!

The conga craze began to spread, and eventually Desi was brought to New York to open a conga club there. This brought him to the attention of Rodgers and Hart, who were casting their new Broadway production, *Too Many Girls*. The story was simple. The girls at Pottawatomie College wear beanies on their heads to let everyone know that they're still virgins. The wealthy father of one of the girls hires four football players to make sure she's still wearing her beanie at the end of the second act.

One of the players is a South American student named Manolito. Lorenz Hart saw Desi at La Conga in Miami and thought he would be perfect in the part, but the ultimate decision was up to the director, George Abbott. (At the writing of this book, George Abbott is about to celebrate his 102nd birthday by starting work on a new show.)

Although Desi had no experience as an actor, Abbott decided his "personality plus" would see him through. The show opened at the Imperial Theatre on October 14, 1939. It was a hit and Desi, doing the conga, stopped the show. The RKO bosses bought the screen rights, and signed Desi to beat the drum for them.

Desi had a crush on the leading lady in New York, and wondered (hoped) history would repeat itself. Desi was polite when he stood up and shook Lucy's hand for the first time, but the horror was etched on his face. Lucy was in her floozy costume, with her makeup plastered on. He couldn't believe this old hooker was going to be the ingenue.

Lucy knew what Desi was thinking and

thought she'd play a trick on him. She changed out of her stripper costume, redid her makeup, and went to the Little Theatre, where Desi was rehearsing, to flirt with him. She knew he wouldn't recognize her, and he didn't. George Abbott passed by as they were talking and said, "I thought you two would get along." Lucy reintroduced herself and shook hands; a foreshadowing of Lucy playing tricks on Ricky? Although they were both dating other people at the time, he told her the cast was going dancing that night. He asked her to go with him, and promised he would teach her to rumba. She accepted. "It wasn't really a date," Lucy said, "it was just the cast going out together—you know, to get to know each other." Lucy and Desi didn't get to know the rest of the cast that night, because they only talked to each other.

"Did you kiss him good night?" (I had to ask.)

"No. He gave me a peck on the cheek, but I didn't let him kiss me. I had his number from the first night, and I wasn't going to make it easy for him."

A few days later, they met again at a party given by Eddie and Connie Bracken. Lucy with there with Hall, Desi with the girl he had been living with in New York. Lucy was playing volleyball when Desi approached her, and they talked. While she was changing out of her bathing suit, Desi sneaked up to the bedroom and took the kiss that Lucille didn't give him a few nights before. When they heard a few of the other girls coming up to change, they hid in a closet. An hour later, they left the dates they had brought and went back to Desi's apartment. Lucy ended her relationship with Al Hall that night, and Desi sent his girl back to New York.

Lucy blushed as she told me the story, and I couldn't let the moment pass. I looked at her and said, "And you weren't going to make it easy for him?!" Lucy knew from the first night that it was Desi she had been looking for. Desi was in love with Lucy, but wouldn't give up his other "bed partners."

While *Too Many Girls* brought them together, too many girls almost tore them apart. "Desi came from a whole different world, where a man was a man and he proved it by the number of women he screwed. His father told him that even if I caught him in bed with another girl to deny it."

Their affair was stormy, the lovemaking as intense as their fights. Lucy didn't want to marry him but knew she couldn't live without him. Six months after they met, Lucy was on tour promoting *Dance, Girl, Dance*, and Desi was appearing with his orchestra at the Roxy Theatre in New York.

"The one thing we found out from being separated was that we couldn't make love on the phone, but we could sure fight." Desi thought Lucy was cheating on him, which Lucy thought was funny. "He's upset because he thinks I'm having an affair, but can't understand why I'm upset because I *know he's* having an affair!"

Lucy remembers how they decided to make the final commitment. "I was in Miami doing promotion for the picture, and Desi called and said come to New York immediately. I asked him why, and he said it was urgent . . . come to New York right away. I remember that I was at the hotel with Harriet, and I packed a bag and ran down to the lobby. I saw Joe Cotten and asked him when I could get a plane. Why I asked Joe Cotten that I'll never know—as if he had the plane schedule. I told Harriet to stay in Miami until I called her, and then I would tell her whether to meet me in New York or go back to California and meet me there. I got out to the airport, and it was raining cats and dogs. It was very late, and the airport was just about shut down. The fellow at the desk told me that there were no more flights for the night. A train would take too long, so I talked one of the pilots into flying me to New York for some astronomical amount of money. I can't remember exactly, but it was a few thousand dollars. What a ride. We bumped all the way to New York, and I got there about six in the morning and checked into the Pierre. I picked up the phone to call Desi, but he didn't tell me where he was. I went over to the Roxy, where he was playing, and waited for him to show up. I asked him what was so important. He told me we were getting married. That's how he proposed. He *told* me we were getting married. I hit the ceiling. How *dare* he tell me. Then I said yes. We went to Woolworth's or someplace like that, and he bought me a cheap ring, and we went up to Greenwich, Connecticut, to get married. We were going to get married in the judge's office, but I think he felt sorry for us, and brought us over to the country club (the Byram River Beagle Club) and did it there. We were back at the Roxy a few hours later and made an entrance together. The audience screamed and yelled. It was terrific. A few hours later, I called Harriet, who I had forgotten all about. She was still in Miami waiting for me to tell her where to go. Harriet answered the phone, and I said, 'Harriet. You'll never guess. I just got married!' Harriet paused for a minute and said, 'Who did *we* marry?' "

Desi thought that a wedding ring was only for a woman. "It was that whole Latin macho stuff," Lucy said. "After we got married, I bought a ring for him to wear, but he refused. He wouldn't put it on his finger, but after a battle, he gave in to a compromise. He put it on a gold chain with a Saint Christopher medal and wore it around his neck."

A friend of Desi's told him about five acres of land, including house, guest house, and orange grove in Northridge. Northridge is a small town in the San Fernando Valley (where Lucy had always objected to the heat) that was for sale for fifteen thousand dollars. A developer was trying to lure the Hollywood crowd out to the area, and practically gave the Arnazes the ranch to get the ball rolling. The area has long since been subdivided, with tract houses, condos, and apartments now standing in the middle of the Desilu ranch.

They put 10 percent down and moved in. "Mary Pickford and Doug Fairbanks had called their place Pickfair, so we came up with Desilu. Desi wanted to call it Lu-Des but I thought it sounded too much like lewdness. Can you imagine, 'Let's go to lewdness for the weekend'?"

Lucy and I went to the scrapbooks, and she showed me a page filled with snapshots she and Desi had taken of each other shortly after moving in. Lucy smiled as she turned the pages looking at the black-and-white prints. Desi hanging off a diving board, his bathing suit barely staying on. Lucy in front of baby orange trees. Desi sunbathing. Lucy working in the garden. These were not publicity pictures. They were pictures of a couple capturing their first married days. No frowns, only smiles.

"We loved to entertain out there," Lucy said. "Our favorite thing to do was have a hoe-down. We'd have a professional caller, and everybody would come out from town and we'd dance all night. You know who enjoyed the square dance more than anyone else in the world? Darryl F. Zanuck. He was a terrific square dancer. He even called pretty well."

While Desi's career was stuck in the mud from lack of Latin parts, Lucy's career was clicking into high gear. In 1941, RKO was about to shoot a script by Billy Wilder and Charles Brackett called *Ball of Fire*. It was the story of a burlesque queen who moves in with eight stuffy college professors to teach them the new "slang" for a new encyclopedia they're writing. The film was a grown-up version of "Snow White and the Seven Dwarfs." Lucy read the script and thought the part was Oscar material. Nobody agreed with her.

Howard Hawks was to direct, and Gary Cooper was set as the male lead, but neither of them thought the movie was anything special. Barbara Stanwyck had been offered the part of the wisecracking stripper but turned it down. Lucy campaigned for the part, tested for it, and got it.

"I did makeup tests, hair tests, and they even had my wardrobe *finished*, when Stanwyck got wind of it and said she would do it. I think the only reason she did the part was because I had it. She was a bigger star and the studio couldn't say no to her, so I was out in left field. I didn't think it was a very nice thing for her to do, but she did it. I'm sure the only reason she changed her mind was because I said yes." The role earned Stanwyck an Oscar nomination.

In 1941, Lucy started work on what was

to be her best role to date, and is considered by some film historians to be her best work ever. The film was called *The Big Street*, and was based on the Damon Runyon story *Little Pinks*. Years later, some of the same satellite characters (Harry the Horse, Nicely-Nicely Johnson, etc.) would show up in the Broadway musical *Guys and Dolls*.

The central character of *The Big Street* was Gloria Lyons, a self-absorbed nightclub singer who cares nothing about anyone or anything but her own career and social advancement. Runyon had final say on the casting, and he was being very particular about who played Gloria. He had already nixed several major stars, but when he met Lucy, he thought she was perfect, and cast her opposite Henry Fonda.

Lucy thought the script was great, but that her character ran the gamut from unlikable to hateful. She sent the script to her friend Charles Laughton, who told her to play it full out. "If you're going to be a bitch, be the bitchiest bitch you can be," Laughton instructed her. "Bitches are more interesting than nice girls anyway." Lucy paid attention.

"I didn't know Henry Fonda all that well before we began, and I sure didn't want to know him all that well when we were finished. He hardly talked to me the whole time, and when he did, well . . ."

Lucy was rattled by Fonda in an incident she never forgot. In the picture, Gloria takes a punch from one of her boyfriends, gets knocked down a flight of stairs, and is left paralyzed from her waist down. In one scene, she's in bed listening to the radio and starts to sway to the music. It's at this moment she realizes that she'll never dance again.

"The director [Irving Reis] and I rehearsed the scene. I started swaying my shoulders, and tried dancing with only my arms. I try to make my legs move, but they won't. I'm dancing, sitting up in the bed, looking at my paralyzed legs. Irving was terrific. He said that I had done it perfectly and he wanted to shoot it right away while we still had the mood. I looked over to the door, and Fonda was standing there. He had watched the rehearsal, and as soon as Irving started setting up the shot, he came over to me and said, 'You're *not* going to do it like that, are you?' I said, 'Well, Irving said it was good.' Fonda just shook his head back and forth and walked away. Try to do a scene after that."

I thought I had hit upon a great psychological motivation for why the scene had turned out so well and asked Lucy, "When you were in bed paralyzed, I'll bet all you thought about was when you had to spend two years in bed as a teenager." Lucy looked at me surprised and said, "I never thought of it once." Lucy made another lifelong friend in that picture, Agnes Moorehead, who some years later lived across the street from Lucy at 1023 North Roxbury.

"I loved Aggie. When *How the West Was Won* came out, I ran to see it, and God was it great. Unbelievable. I called all my friends and told them to rush to see it. I went over to Aggie's house and asked her if she had seen the film, and she said no. I went on and on about it and told her that she had to drop whatever she was doing and see the best movie of all time. Well, about two weeks later, I saw Aggie and said, 'Have you seen *How the West Was Won?* I've seen it twice now.' Aggie shook her head and said, 'No, I haven't seen it yet.' I got so frustrated with her, I shouted 'Why? I told you to go see it. I begged you to go see it. Don't you believe me when I tell you it's good? Now why haven't you seen it?' Aggie looked at me like I was a first-class dope and said,

'Because I'm *in* it!' Aggie had played Debbie Reynolds' mother, and she was so god-damned brilliant that I never recognized her."

After *The Big Street,* there were no pictures in the immediate future. Desi was back on the road with his band, and back in New York for an engagement. "I went there to meet him. I knew he was fooling around with somebody, and I couldn't do anything about it long distance. Also, I knew I couldn't get pregnant over the telephone. I wanted to be pregnant. New York was fun, and we were having a great time. One Sunday, we were at a friend's apartment overlooking Central Park West, and we were in bed listening to the football game. It was about one in the afternoon or so, and all of a sudden it came over the radio—the Japanese had attacked Pearl Harbor. That changed everything. We left for the ranch the next morning, hoping that it would still be there."

CHAPTER
Eight

ONE AFTERNOON I arrived at the usual time, but Lucy wasn't ready for me. She was in her little beauty parlor having her hair done. Gary and I sat in the lanai making plans for an upcoming meeting at Twentieth Century-Fox. After about ten minutes, Lucy ran into the room in a short white robe. Her hair was soaking wet and dropping ringlets around her face. "I'm sorry. Irma was late. I'll be right back. I'm having my hair dyed."

Gary shouted as she was halfway out the door, "What color are you having it done?"

Lucy looked over her shoulder as she kept going and gave him a dirty look along with her answer. "Red!" Gary and I howled. It was such a silly question, and she was so serious. What other color would Lucy's hair be but red?

Lucy told me she admired Clara Bow so much that she wanted to have her red hair. She dyed it herself, and didn't always match the color exactly. This was particularly disconcerting when she did it during the shooting of a film. Although the movie was in black and white, it was obvious that Lucy had two different hair shades from scene to scene.

When Lucy came back in from the little beauty parlor, her hair was up in curlers. She put a portable dryer on her head as we sat down to play. It was a blue plastic contraption that looked like the oat bag she wore in a Paris *I Love Lucy* episode in which Ricky fooled her into thinking it was a chic designer hat.

Lucy said that her red hair color had almost come to an abrupt end in 1952 because King Farouk of Egypt had been overthrown. I didn't see the connection, and asked her why. She said, "I got all of my henna rinse from Cairo. It was the real thing, and it was imported. When they overthrew Farouk, they stopped importing it. All I knew was that I couldn't get it anymore. My hair was starting to go two-tone like a De Soto. Well, one night I was at a party, and the ex-Egyptian ambassador was there. I told him my predicament, and he said I shouldn't worry. He knew where he could get the henna I loved and would send me some. About a week later, a man came to the door and said he had a delivery. It was the henna rinse powder. A full TON of it! He brought in carton after carton after carton. We stacked it in the garage. There's still some left. There'll be henna rinse powder in the garage until the turn of the century."

Shortly after Lucy dyed her hair bright red, a friend stopped her on the lot and said,

"Nobody has that shade of hair." Lucy said, "I do."

When Lucy and Desi first got married, they only had the pressures of work keeping them apart; now, the war added to their separation. Desi first accepted a commission as a lieutenant in the Cuban Army, but traded it to be a seaman in the U.S. Navy. The navy rejected him. He was not a citizen at the time, although he had applied for his naturalization papers. The law was that as a resident alien he could be drafted but could not volunteer.

Desi was signed to another picture, *Four Jacks and a Jill*, where he fought continuously with Jack Hively, the director. His next assignment was as a sailor in *The Navy Comes Through*. Ironically, he could play a sailor, but he couldn't be one.

With film parts coming few and far between for young Latin men, Desi threw himself into building up the ranch. They planted more orange trees and grape orchards and bought some livestock in order to be more self-sufficient. During this time, a young female fell in love with Desi, and there was nothing Lucy could do about it. The Duchess lived at the Desilu ranch and was crazy for Desi. "One night," Lucy related, "the

Duchess came in the house, right into the bedroom, and tried to get into Desi's side of the bed with him." The Duchess was a two-thousand-pound cow!

Desi was restless because of not being able to do his share to win the war, so he volunteered to travel with the USO shows. He was on the road again, but this time it was for Uncle Sam.

Lucy was doing her share of USO tours separately from Desi. She was nervous traveling without him. "I had such fear about flying after Carole Lombard was killed. Carole and Gable were friends. They lived near us in the Valley and would come over for dinner and games. She was so pretty and so much fun. I never knew what she saw in Gable. He was handsome all right, but he was such a lump. She died only a few weeks after Pearl Harbor. To me, she was the war's first casualty."

Lucy asked to be given a train tour, but the combination of stars was pulling in big bucks for the government, which didn't want to break it up. Lucy thought about Carole Lombard whenever she got on a plane. "We went from city to city by air. We had Betty Grable and Harry James, Marie McDonald (nicknamed "the Body"),

Ann Sheridan, and Frank Fay." (Fay was a well-known character actor who would make a hit on Broadway in the 1946 play *Harvey* by Mary Chase. His replacement in the role made an even bigger hit, a fellow named James Stewart.)

Lucy thought about Frank Fay and said, "He had to be one of the most obnoxious men who ever lived. Nobody in town liked him. I don't even know why he was on the tour with us. Fay lusted after Marie McDonald like nothing I've ever seen. Boy, did he want that woman. But he went about it in the most disgusting ways possible. He would back her into a corner and say to her, 'I'm going to fuck you.' Or he'd call her hotel room in the middle of the night and say, 'I'd love to see the back of your belly.' Marie just hated him and avoided him like the plague, but Frank did everything he could to be near her. One night we were all taking the plane to the next city on the tour and Frank was sitting across the aisle from Marie—leering at her. Suddenly, we hit the worst turbulence I ever felt in my life, and the plane was all over the sky. Up and down. Up and down. I was sure we were going to crash. All I could think of was Carole. I looked over at Marie bouncing around in her seat with her big tits going up and down and everybody's screaming except Frank Fay, who can't get his eyes off Marie's tits. She was clutching the arm rest, and her face was white as a sheet. She looked over at Frank and said, 'So you want to fuck me?' Fay shook his head yes. McDonald grabbed him and said, 'Okay . . . NOW!'"

Lucy left RKO and went to MGM, where she starred in *DuBarry Was a Lady. DuBarry* was a first-class picture; the big screen, Technicolor version of Cole Porter's Broadway musical that had starred Bert Lahr and Lucy's old friend Ethel Merman. While she was filming it, Lucy had an extraordinary experience that might have changed the outcome of the war!

She talked about the incident one afternoon after a particularly painful visit to the dentist. "It was a terrible time in California. The Japanese-Americans had been sent to the camps at Manzanar, and everyone was very edgy about everybody else. They had spotted a Japanese submarine off of Santa Barbara, and somebody even saw a Japanese Zero flying over Santa Monica. Well, I was having some dental work done, and the dentist put in some temporary fillings while he worked on the permanent ones. At that time, they used lead for the temps, and I had several of them done, both upper and lower. I was shooting *DuBarry* at MGM and living at the ranch, which was about a thirty-five-mile drive. We were shooting very late, and the drive wasn't pleasant. One night I came into the Valley over Coldwater Canyon, and I heard music. I reached down to turn the radio off, and it wasn't on. The music kept getting louder and louder, and then I realized it was coming from my mouth. I even recognized the tune. My mouth was humming and thumping with the drum-beat, and I thought I was losing my mind. I thought, What the hell is this? Then it started to subside. I got home and went to bed, not sure if I should tell anybody what had happened because they would think I was crazy. The next day I ran into Buster Keaton at the studio, and I mentioned it to him. It didn't seem to faze him a bit. He asked me if I was at Moorpark and Coldwater. I was astounded. I told him that's exactly where I was. He said, 'Do you have any fillings?' Again, I was astounded. I told him I had some temporary fillings. He laughed and said it had happened to another friend of his. I was picking up the radio station in my teeth. Well, I couldn't wait to go by the street again to see what else I could pick up. The next night I drove past the spot, and nothing happened. The station was off the air. I was really disappointed. I went by every night, and it still didn't happen. Then one night about five nights later, I took a different street. It was right near four vacant lots where they had torn down some buildings in order to put up the Birmingham Hospital. All of a sudden, my mouth started jumping. It wasn't music this time, it was Morse code. It started softly, and then de-de-de-de-de-de. As soon as it started fading, I stopped the car and then started backing up until it was coming in full strength. DE-DE-DE-DE-DE-DE DE-DE-DE-DE! I tell you, I got the hell out of there real quick. The next day I told the MGM Security Office about it, and they called the FBI or something, and sure enough, they found an underground Japanese radio station. It was somebody's gardener, but sure enough, they were spies. I always thought, Would we have lost the war if I had been born with good teeth?"

Lucy told the story to Ethel Merman, who told Cole Porter, who put it into the plot of their next show, *Something for the Boys.*

Lucy's next assignment was a real stretch. She was signed to play herself in another

Broadway transfer, *Best Foot Forward*. Lucy, as Lucille needing publicity, accepts a cadet's invitation to his military prom without knowing that he has a very jealous girlfriend who hates the idea. I looked through Lucy's video library one day and saw that she didn't have a copy of the film. I had one, and asked her if she'd like one. "What on earth would I want that for?"

During the war years, Desi saw more action in bed than he did on the battlefield. RKO dropped his option after three pictures, and he accepted a job in a Ken Murray revue. Louis B. Mayer saw the show, and signed Desi to a contract at MGM. He was on tour with the Hollywood Victory Caravan when he finally got drafted. Having had two knee operations as a teenager, he was not given active duty. The closest he came to battle was playing a soldier in the film *Bataan,* where he didn't even get to die in battle. He died of malaria three quarters of the way through the picture.

Desi was sent to the now-completed Birmingham Hospital (the site where Lucy's fillings discovered the Japanese spies) as entertainment director. It was Desi's job to organize the activities and shows at the hospital for the returning wounded soldiers.

Desi spent more time at the hospital than Lucy thought he should have. "Instead of providing extracurricular activities for the men, he was providing them for himself." Believing he was involved with every nurse at the hospital, Lucy moved out of the Desilu ranch and into an apartment in Beverly Hills.

Lucy formally filed for divorce in 1944. The night before she was to go to court, Desi called her and suggested they have dinner together. Lucy accepted. He begged her not to go through with it. She told him that she had no choice. The press would be at court, and she couldn't call it off at this point. She would go easy on him. After the quick hearing, she was granted the divorce, and then went back to the apartment, where Desi was waiting for her. They spent the next few days in bed together.

At that time, California law dictated that if a couple cohabitated before the divorce was final, it was invalid. Their marriage still had sixteen years to go.

When the war ended, Lucy was working constantly in pictures; Desi was not. He was still under contract to MGM, but the Latin lover roles for which he was right were few and far between. Desi saw the handwriting on the wall and decided to leave MGM before he was fired. He went to Mayer, who released him from his contract, and reformed his orchestra. They opened at Ciro's, one of Hollywood's most popular nightclubs, where Desi revived the conga and added a new song to his repertory . . . "Babalu"!

This new arrangement added another glitch to the newly saved Arnaz marriage. Lucy was making picture after picture at MGM, while Desi was making a hit at Ciro's. Their schedules were completely opposite. Lucy would have to be in hair and makeup at the Culver City studios at 6:00 A.M. Desi didn't finish at Ciro's until 4:00 A.M., and would be going home when Lucy was going to work. They would meet at the top of Coldwater Canyon at Mulholland Drive and spend a few minutes with each other before each went his separate way.

(When I would drive to Lucy's house every afternoon, I took the same route over Coldwater. There is a small area for cars to pull off the road, and I often thought about Lucy and Desi parking there, necking, as I passed it.)

When Lucy wasn't making a picture, she would spend the time with Desi at Ciro's. On nights they both had off, they would entertain at the ranch. "We loved Hollywood charades," Lucy told me.

I didn't know what Hollywood charades was, and asked if you had to live in Hollywood or be a star to play.

She explained: "Hollywood charades is great. It's more active than regular charades. You break into two teams and separate—one team in one part of the house, the other team at the other end of the house. Each person writes six things to guess. You know—book titles, movie titles, the usual stuff, only short. You couldn't write anything over four words to guess. One person (called the holder) would take the titles and stand at a halfway point in the center of the house between the two teams. One representative of each team would get the subject from the holder, then run back to his own team and act it out. Whoever guessed it right would run back to the teller and get the next subject and do it all over again. There was a lot of running involved. One night, I'll never forget, we had Keenan and Evie Wynn, Laird Cregar, my sister, Cleo [Cleo was actually Lucy's first cousin, but she never referred to her as anything but her sister] and her husband Ken, Francis Lederer, and a few other people. I don't think we ever laughed so much. All that running and jumping. Laird Cregar was terrific. A big guy with piercing eyes, he loved games and was so good. And a great actor! He won that night. We were all covered with sweat, so the bunch of us jumped in the pool for a midnight swim. The next day I was driving to the studio, and I heard that Laird had died of a heart attack that night. I almost drove right off the road. He must have died as soon as he got home. We all felt terrible. I couldn't ever play Hollywood charades again without thinking about him."

Lucy reminisced about the ranch. "We always had people around. Lionel Barrymore was a good friend of ours. He was getting old and would come out and stay in our guest house for a day, and then a weekend, and then he was pretty much living there. He brought a cat with him, and then another cat, and soon we had cats all over the place. Desi and I had Junior [a German shepherd] at the time, and the cats used to drive poor Junior crazy. One night, it was very late, Desi and I had a fire going, and it seemed like the smoke from the fireplace was coming into the room. We thought it was the flue. Desi got up to open it and saw that the smoke was *not* coming from the fireplace but through an open window. He looked out and saw that the guest house was on fire. Lionel was still inside. He had set the little cottage on fire by careless smoking. I got a hose, which didn't seem to be doing much good, and Desi ran into the flames to take Lionel out. Lionel wouldn't go without the cats. Desi picked him up and carried him out. Lionel was screaming to put him down. He wouldn't leave without the animals. But Desi just picked up the poor old guy and carried him out. A lot of animals died that night. I don't even want to think about it."

Lucy and Desi were trying very hard to have children. She found out she was pregnant in early 1946, but miscarried a few weeks later. She turned back to her work to alleviate the pain. Although she was making picture after picture at MGM, none of them "took off." Still, she was honored by the Hollywood press club by being named the 1946 "Queen of Comedy." Danny Kaye was named "King of Comedy." Lucy made a switch to Columbia, where she would be working under another king, Harry Cohn, the most disliked man in Hollywood.

While she was working at Columbia, Lucy started a radio series, *My Favorite Husband*, with Richard Denning. She was happy doing comedy in front of a live audience, and unhappy that Desi was on the road. She couldn't get pregnant alone. Desi's Latin orchestra was a big success. He was finally making big money.

Lucy had an offer that she refused at first but then reconsidered. A young actor turned producer named Herbert Kenwith called Lucy and asked her to come East to star in a stock version of Elmer Rice's play *Dream Girl*. "I didn't know what I wanted to do, but Desi was always gone and I liked the idea of working in front of an audience, so I thought, why not." The director was Kenwith's partner, Harold J. Kennedy. Years later, Kenwith himself would direct several seasons of *The Lucy Show*.

Lucy accepted the show because it would play Princeton, New Jersey, about an hour's drive from New York City, where Desi was appearing at the Copa with his orchestra. Lucy played the role of Georgina Allerton, a lady who finds her fantasy life more appealing than her real one. It was the largest part written for a woman up to that time. Said Lucy, "Somebody once told me that it was longer than Hamlet."

The show was an immediate hit. One of the scrapbooks that Lucy kept was filled with all the *Dream Girl* reviews. She even saved the ads announcing the show. With *Dream Girl* being a big hit, Kenwith and Kennedy asked Lucy to tour with it. There was nothing immediate coming up for her at Columbia, so she agreed on one condition: that the show play Los Angeles. She wanted the people out there to see she could act.

The Los Angeles notices were love letters to Lucy. The critics praised her as a great comic actress. One night during a performance, Lucy collapsed onstage. She said, "I don't know why, but I always got sick when I was in a show. I wonder what that means?" I told her I thought it meant she wanted out of the show and got sick instead of breaking the contract. She told me to go back to interpreting dreams.

Lucy was halfhearted about her work. For the first time in her life, she didn't care about the next part or the next film. All she cared about was having a baby.

CHAPTER
Nine

EVERY DAY AT three o'clock, Lucy and I would continue playing backgammon, but we'd be joined by Oprah Winfrey . . . on TV. Lucy enjoyed her show very much. About five minutes to three, she would say, "It's almost time for Okra!" One day the subject of the program was women who had children in their forties. Lucy's ears perked up. The women discussed their fears about having children late in life. Lucy could identify. Some were married, and some were "liberated women" who wanted to have children without being burdened by husbands.

I asked Lucy how she felt about "women's liberation." She clucked, "I was always liberated. I'm so liberated I can't stand it. I know a lot of men who aren't liberated. It's not just a women's thing. I always did what I wanted to and was paid pretty well for it. Mostly, I wanted to perform and have children, and that's all. Desi was the businessman. He did all the building. He was the genius behind things. Desi revolutionized television. But even when he was doing all the building, people wouldn't believe it was him doing it. I got a lot of credit I didn't deserve. Desi suffered a lot by that. Because he was a Cuban and a bongo player, they called him 'spick' and every name in the book; names he didn't deserve. Hell, I never wanted to be the breadwinner. I always

125

wanted somebody to lean on. The only problem was that Desi was hardly ever there to lean on. He was on the road with the band."

In the late forties, Lucy was more determined to get pregnant than anything else. Her contract at Columbia was coming to an end, and she could accept projects that didn't interfere with having a child. When William Paley called Lucy to ask her to bring *My Favorite Husband* to television, she told him she was going on the road with Desi because she wanted to have a baby. She couldn't do a television show without him. She suggested that if Desi played her husband on the show, then they'd be able to be together. Paley said it was a silly idea, out of the question, but wished her well.

Lucy was not happy at Columbia, and Harry Cohn was not happy with her. Still, she was signed to Cohn for one more picture, for which she would receive eighty-five thousand dollars. Lucy didn't want to break her contract; she wanted the eighty-five thousand dollars.

Lucy had a call from Cecil B. deMille at Paramount, who wanted her to play the "Elephant Girl" in a picture called *The Greatest Show on Earth*. Lucy wanted to work with the legendary deMille desperately, and Cohn knew it. He also knew about deMille's offer, and waited for Lucy to come and ask to be let out of her contract. Lucy never came.

Cohn sent her a script that he was sure she would refuse to do; a terrible costume quickie called *The Magic Carpet*. Lucy read the script and shuddered. It was what they called a contract breaker; if you refused the terrible picture, your contract was broken.

About the same time, Lucy found out that she was again pregnant. She told only Desi. He wanted her to break the Columbia contract by refusing *The Magic Carpet*, but Lucy thought if they started the picture on time, she'd be finished before her pregnancy showed, and they'd be eighty-five thousand dollars the better for it. She didn't think the picture would hurt her career, because she couldn't imagine anyone paying to see it.

Lucy shot the picture, and to the wardrobe mistress's dismay, Lucy's harem costume was getting tighter and tighter every day. She kept saying "I have to go on a diet." Lucy's costar was an old friend, Raymond Burr. He, too, knew he was in a stinker and wanted to get through it as fast as possible.

Lucy was expected on the set of *The Greatest Show on Earth*, but knew she couldn't hide the pregnancy any longer. She went to see Mr. deMille. "I told him that I wanted to do the picture, but that I was going to have a baby. He told me to have an abortion. Imagine that! I'd been trying to have a child for years, and he tells me to have an abortion. The picture was more important to him than the baby. I told Desi, and he went through the ceiling. I thought he was going to go over to Paramount and punch deMille right in the mouth. The picture went on as scheduled, and Gloria Grahame got the part. We didn't want the world to know just yet that I was pregnant, because I had a miscarriage before and I didn't know what was going to happen. When the word got out, Harry Cohn realized that I was pregnant during the filming of *The Magic Carpet* and called me every name in the book.

"Later we were at some party somewhere, and Desi saw deMille. He was still furious with him for suggesting that I have an abortion. DeMille came over to Desi and shook his hand and said, 'Congratulations!' Desi thought he was going to apologize for his hard-heartedness, but deMille continued, 'You're the only man to fuck Harry Cohn, Cecil B. deMille, Paramount Pictures, and Lucille Ball all at the same time.' Desi had to laugh."

Lucy lost the baby, and tried again to get pregnant immediately. She knew she could bear children because of the previous conceptions, but still listened to everyone's advice about how to get pregnant. She was trying hot baths, cold showers, body-temperature checks, exotic positions, and any old wives' tale remotely related to the subject of pregnancy.

At the time, Lucy was a friend of Betty Garrett and her husband, Larry Parks. One day, while driving down Sunset Boulevard, Lucy stopped for a red light, and Betty Garrett pulled up next to her. They were both in convertibles. Betty shouted to Lucy, "I'm pregnant!"

Lucy scrunched up her face and shook her fists. "You bum! I hate you! Congratulations! What should I do? Tell me what you did."

Betty said, "You *know* what we did!"

Lucy said, "Yeah. But then what? Herbal tea? Pickles?"

Betty yelled to Lucy that after intercourse, she should lie on the bed with her feet placed high up on the wall for about an hour. Lucy thanked her for the suggestion. As the light turned green, the two stars noticed that everybody around them had heard the whole conversation.

Desi's mother, Dolores, had her own opinion of why the marriage was without children. A devout Roman Catholic, she told Lucy that God had not blessed the union because they had not been married in the Church. Dolores believed that Lucy wouldn't have had the miscarriages if she had not eloped. Dolores promised Lucy would carry a child to term if they were married by a priest. Lucy herself was not religious, but she was willing to try anything. The idea of a Church wedding grew on her. The thought of it was very romantic to Lucy, and she "knew" she would get pregnant when the priest made her promise she would "raise the children Catholic." Lucy laughed. "He said it with such authority. Like he knew there *would* be children, and we *would* raise them as Catholics." Lucy and Desi were remarried in a Roman Catholic church in the Valley, with Dolores looking on, smiling.

(Dolores Arnaz died at the age of ninety-one only a few months before Lucy. She lived in a nursing home and was quite senile. Despite the fact that she never recognized her, Lucie Arnaz visited her grandmother often.)

In the meantime, Lucy got another call from Bill Paley, who said that Desi might have a small role in the show if that was what she wanted. Lucy told him Desi should play her husband, but Paley thought it was a bad idea. He didn't think anyone would believe a Cuban married to a Scotch-Irish girl. Paley would have to think it over.

Lucy gave him something to think about. She suggested to Desi that they do an act together and take it on the road. In the summer of 1950, Lucy joined Desi on a cross-country tour so that the public would connect them as a married couple.

CBS was beginning to accept the idea of a Lucy-Desi series. After Lucy's death, William Paley gave an interview to Dan Rather in which he spoke of the beginnings of *I Love Lucy*. He said, "We gave in to Lucy about Desi. We gave him a small part, but before we knew it he had a larger part and a larger part, and then his part was as big as hers and almost as important, and then he was producing the show, and then he became one of the best comedy producers in Hollywood. He was a real talent, and it wouldn't have come to the surface if it weren't for her persistence."

Lucy found out she was pregnant once again. She agreed to make a pilot for the series, because it was still early in the pregnancy. They used the act they had done on the road and based the pilot around it.

Lucy was not going to take any chances with the new pregnancy. She was almost forty years old, and knew that there wouldn't be many more chances to have children. She went to bed at the ranch to take it easy while Desi plunged into putting the show together. She did make the occasional phone call to help. Lucy insisted on hiring the same writers who had worked on *My Favorite Husband* and on casting two of her favorite actors to play the parts of Fred and Ethel Mertz. She wanted Gale Gordon and Bea Benaderet. Neither was available; Gordon was playing Osgood Conklin on the radio show *Our Miss Brooks* starring Eve Arden, and Benaderet was playing Blanche Morton on *The Burns and Allen Show*.

Desi had many obstacles to overcome, and one by one he overcame them all. The CBS brass wanted the show done in New York so it could be kinescoped to the West Coast. Lucy had two requirements. She wanted the show done on film. She said, "I never took the whole thing that seriously. I thought it would be nice for the kids we were going to have to see some home movies. I wanted my kids to see them as they were done. Kinescopes looked like they were shot through linoleum." Lucy also wanted to do it in front of a live audience. Paley said she couldn't have it both ways. Desi contacted Karl Freund, who was one of the great cinematographers, and challenged him to solve the problem. Desi had the idea to film in front of three cameras and edit; Karl executed the idea.

Since Gale Gordon and Bea Benaderet were both unavailable, the Mertzes still had to be cast. "My second choice for Fred," Lucy told me, "was Jimmy Gleason. We had worked together at RKO. He was a good actor and easy to work with. Jimmy wasn't well at the time and begged off. Bill Frawley called me to say he was available, and Desi went to meet him."

Frawley had a reputation as a big boozer, and Desi was afraid to take the chance on him. He thought he was perfect for the part after they met at Nickodell's restaurant, and Desi hired Frawley on one condition. If Frawley ever missed a day of work because of drinking, he was out. Frawley agreed, and never missed one day.

Lucy was feeling terrific about life. She knew the pregnancy was "right" and would come to full term. She had terrible morning sickness and loved every minute of it. She could feel the baby growing and kicking inside her, and she was happier than she'd ever been in her life. As the date approached, Lucy and Desi sat up at night discussing names for the child. Finally, they decided to call the baby Susan if it was a girl and Desiderio if it was a boy.

Lucy went into the hospital, and a girl was born by cesarean section on July 17, 1951. Lucy was to receive a big shock when she woke up from the anesthesia. "I came around and asked the nurse if it was a boy or a girl. She told me it was a beautiful, healthy girl. I said, 'Susan. I want to see Susan.' The nurse looked at me as if I were nuts, and said, 'Who's Susan?' I said, 'My daughter. My Susan.' She said, 'You mean Lucie?' I said, 'I'm Lucy. I want Susan.' While I was asleep, Desi signed the birth certificate and called her Lucie. All on his own."

The first time Lucille was allowed to hold her daughter was almost an *I Love Lucy* episode in itself. She told me she was sitting up in the bed, and her abdomen was killing her. The doctors had just sewn her up, and it hurt to move in any direction. A nurse brought Lucie in around feeding time and showed her how to hold the bottle. Lucy remembers, "I didn't breast-feed her. I don't know why, I guess it wasn't all that popular back then, but the nurse showed me how to hold her in one arm and feed her with the other. She asked me if I needed anything, and I told her no, I just wanted to be alone with my new baby. She put the bottle down on the end table and left me alone with Lucie. I kept looking at her and looking at her, and I just couldn't believe it. Talk about a miracle. The child I had wanted and waited for so long was at last in my arms. Here I am, treasuring the moment, and she started to cry just a little bit. So I reached for the bottle, but the nurse had placed it on the table so it was just out of reach. My stitches were hurting, and the more I reached for the bottle with one hand, the more I could feel Lucie slipping out of my other arm. The button to call the nurse was on the same side I was holding Lucie, so I knew that wouldn't work. Lucie kept slipping and slipping, and I thought, My God, I'm going to drop her right on the floor. I gritted my teeth and gave her a hoist to get a better hold on her, and wham! Up she went. I threw her right over my shoulder. Thank God there was a headboard. That's where she landed. If there hadn't been a headboard, I might have thrown her right out the window. We were doing shtick together, and she wasn't even a day old."

Now that Lucy's baby was born and healthy, she was hungry to work again. With a week to go before shooting, they were still without an actress to play Ethel Mertz. The director of the show was Marc Daniels, and the head writer was Jess Oppenheimer. (In an ironic twist of fate, Lucy, Marc, and Jess all died within three weeks of each other.) Marc suggested a friend of his named Vivian Vance. She was a stage actress, which was what they wanted, because of the decision to film the show like a play.

Vivian was appearing in John Van Druten's play *The Voice of the Turtle* at the La Jolla Playhouse near San Diego. Lucy was at Desilu with Lucie when Marc, Jess, and Desi went to see a performance and hired Vivian. Desi worried all the way back that he had made a mistake. What if Lucy couldn't stand Vivian? He didn't have to concern himself. When the two girls met, they not only became close coworkers, they became best girlfriends offscreen as well.

As Lucy told us at a Sherwood Oaks class, Bill Frawley and Vivian hated each other. She said it started the first day of rehearsal. Vivian was shocked when she met Bill and saw that he was old enough to be her father. He overheard her say during a break in the first rehearsal, "How can anyone believe that I'm married to that old coot?" Frawley never forgave her for that remark.

Lucy always grew misty when she spoke about Vivian. "Vivian and I were inseparable. When she was married to Phil Ober, she . . . God, that man!"

"What's the matter with him?" I wanted to know.

"He was a terrible man. He used to beat her up. Loved to embarrass her. He was nuts, and he made her nuts. She was seeing all these shrinks. God, it was a mess. I told her year after year to get rid of the guy, but if Vivian was one thing, it was loyal. She asked us to use him on the show, and we gave him a couple of bit parts, but he wasn't fun to have around. He got scary."

Lucy got angry as she told this story. "One day Viv came to work with a shiner. That

137

did it. I think I said to her, 'If you don't divorce him, I will.' And she did. She married John Dodds, who was a book publisher and a very sweet man. Her second marriage was very happy. I think second marriages are always happier. But Viv was so happy, she didn't want to work anymore. When she found her perfect partner, I lost mine."

Vivian would often be at the house. "One Sunday afternoon, Viv came over and we were doing our hair. We used to play "beauty parlor" like two idiots. We were like two teenagers, and we'd have a couple of drinks and play games . . . you know, the usual stuff. Suddenly, there was a knock at the door. Since it was Sunday, the staff was off, and Desi was fishing in Del Mar, and Vivian and I were all by ourselves. I didn't want to answer the door, but they kept knocking and knocking, and I went to the window and twelve limousines were lined up and motorcycles and police cars with flashing lights, and Viv and I are dripping wet. I opened the door, and people came running in, led by the Beverly Hills Chamber of Commerce. It was the nawab of Brunei or the sheik of Araby or the sultan of Swat. I didn't know who the hell he was except that he was a head of state and all he wanted to do was see where Lucy and Ricky lived. Here's Vivian and me with towels on our heads and people are running around taking pictures. The man from the chamber of commerce was very apologetic, and said that it was an unscheduled stop. That's an understatement! The king looked all around the lanai, the den, the kitchen, and then he looked at me and asked where Lucy was. I told him she was gone for the day, but I would be sure to tell her that he had stopped by. The entourage bowed their way out the door, and I slammed it behind them. Vivian was rolling on the floor holding herself. She couldn't stop laughing. The king hadn't recognized either one of us. She said that we should use the incident as an episode for the show, but I said that I didn't think anyone would believe it."

It was but one adventure that Lucy and Vivian had together in real life. After *I Love Lucy* debuted on October 15, 1951, they would have over two hundred half-hour adventures together.

CHAPTER
Ten

ON SATURDAY, NOVEMBER 5, 1988, about ten o'clock, the phone rang. It was Lucy. "I know you have plans for this afternoon, but do you think you can change them? I need you." That's all I had to hear. "Come over for lunch?" I said I would be there. It was unusual for Lucy to sound so pleading. I knew Gary was in Palm Springs playing golf, but Lucy was not one to beg for company just because she had to spend an afternoon alone. It turned out to be a very emotional day.

When I got to the house a few hours later, Lucy was done up, almost as if she were going to make a personal appearance. She had eye shadow and a second helping of mascara (which was unusual), and her hair had just been set. She wore a hot-pink running suit. On the jacket pocket of the suit was scripted in black, LUCY WHO She looked great; she was very nervous.

She kissed me when I came in. "Thank you for coming over. I really needed you today."

140

"What's up?"

"The Starlight Foundation called last week. There's a little boy who's dying of leukemia. His last wish is to meet me. How can I say no to that? I just hope I don't disappoint him."

"How could you do that?"

"Just by the way I look. I might scare him. These kids see me one way on television, and then when they meet me, they say, 'Who's that?' God, I hate getting old." The tears were already welling up.

I thought about an interview I once saw with Vicki Lawrence, Carol Burnett's side-kick. Her children were devout Lucy fans, and watched her reruns every afternoon. When her kids saw her new sitcom, *Life with Lucy*, they turned to their mother and said, "She looks better in the afternoon." The Lucy in the afternoon was the one she thought this boy would be expecting, and she didn't want to let him down.

She asked Roza to make us a couple of sandwiches. We sat in Gary's den and had lunch. That room had the best view of the street. Lucy would take a bite and then jump up, run to the window, and check for the car.

"Will you light someplace!" I said to her. She laughed.

"I don't want to answer the door with a piece of chicken hanging out of my mouth."

"Why not?" I said. "You'll start off with a laugh!"

"Yeah, well."

A few minutes later, while she was looking out the window, she saw the limo pull up. You would have thought the president was about to step out.

"He's here. He's here." She didn't know what to do first.

"Do you want me to get the door?"

"No. I'll get it."

She looked through the peephole as the boy and his parents walked up the driveway. I watched from the hall, where I could see Lucy. She took a few deep breaths, pulled her shoulders back, put on a big smile, and opened the door.

"Hi, I'm Lucy. Welcome to my house, John."

She shouldn't have worried about letting the boy down. His pale face lit up when he saw her. John handed her a bouquet of flowers as he entered. She took the flowers and welcomed the family as old friends. She introduced me to them and said, "Let's go into the den, I have some lemonade ready."

She brought the boy and his parents into the lanai. I backed off into the living room, where I could watch and still give them some privacy. Lucy poured the lemonade for the three of them, and I wondered why she wanted to punish those nice people with that lousy lemonade. The boy's father visibly jumped when he took his first gulp. Lucy proposed a toast, and thanked them for taking the time to visit.

"I'm very happy that you wanted to meet me," she told John. "It makes me *very* happy. Well, what would you like to do?"

He had his answer without hesitation. "I want to watch *I Love Lucy* with you." Lucy complied immediately. She went to the den, pulled several cassettes off a shelf, and brought them back. She knew instinctively what episodes the boy was going to ask for.

Lucy hated watching reruns of *I Love Lucy* on television, because of the choppy way they had been edited. She enjoyed watching them if they were complete, the way they had been filmed. At least five minutes of every show had been cut to conform to the standard of today's syndication. In other words, more time was needed for commercials. It drove Lucy up the wall. Several times when I would turn the show on, she would get angry. "The payoff of this scene doesn't make any sense because they cut out the setup."

Lucy thought back to the origins of the show, and said they had no idea what they were doing. They thought the show might last a season, and that would be it. There was no such thing as reruns, so the idea of the show running continuously for almost forty years never entered her mind.

Within three weeks of going on the air, *I Love Lucy* was the number-one show on television. Even today, *I Love Lucy* is being shown somewhere in the world at every minute of the day.

Lucy never considered that the show was about her. She felt that it was a show about marriage and the battle of the sexes. When the show was first conceived, it was very close to who Lucy and Desi really were: a famous band leader and his famous actress-wife. "I just didn't think people could relate to that. The general public doesn't think that movie stars have any problems. They think it's just party after party. But everybody wants to be in show business like Lucy did, and they could relate to that. They could also relate to a husband and wife trying to make it on a budget. That's the way we went. The writers even included a lot of things that were really about me. My name was not McGillicuddy, but I did come from Jamestown, and we used that. I did have friends from there named Marion Strong and Carolyn Appleby and Hal King, and we used all of their names. It added reality."

Lucy enjoyed telling behind-the-scenes stories of the show. The pale little boy listened in awe as Lucy told him story after story.

"When we did the candy factory episode, we wanted to get a real candy dipper. Somebody who worked on the show lived near the Farmer's Market on Fairfax Avenue. Whenever he passed by, he saw a lady dipping candy in the window and thought she was the most deadpan thing he'd ever seen in his life. Her name was Amanda Milligan, and she agreed to do the show. The only thing that this woman ever did her whole life was dip candy. I don't think she ever watched television, and she didn't have the faintest idea who the hell I was. We explained the scene to her a couple of times, and she thought we were all crazy. She never cracked a smile once. We all began to think, Is this funny or isn't it? We told her that I would see a fly land on her nose, and when I knocked the fly off her nose, she should turn and whack me. We rehearsed it without the chocolate on our hands, and Amanda just didn't get it. I hit her, and she tapped me. I tried it again, and she tapped me again. She wouldn't give me the whack I needed to get the laugh. We hoped for the best when we filmed. We started the scene, and there was Amanda dipping the chocolate the way she had for the last thirty years. Well, it came time for me to hit her, which I did, and then for her to hit me . . . which she did! Bam! She gave me such a shot, I thought she had broken my nose. I really saw stars. I almost called for a cut, and then I thought, no we'd have to do it again, so I kept on going. But Lord, did she bust me in the face. After the show, I said, 'Boy you really hit me,' and she looked at me deadpan as ever and said, 'That's what you wanted, wasn't it?' "

Lucy almost drowned in another episode. "We were doing the show where we're in Italy and the director wants me for his picture called *Bitter Grapes*. He wants me for the part of an American tourist, but I think he wants me for a grape stomper, so I go to learn how to stomp grapes. The whole show was geared to get me in that grape vat. Everything that we did on the show we wanted to be authentic, so we looked around for someone who knew how to stomp grapes. Most of the wineries were all mechanized, but we heard there were a few women up near Victorville who still crushed grapes the old-fashioned way. We brought one of the ladies down. Her name was Theresa, and she spoke no English whatsoever. We had a translator on the set and he would tell her what we wanted, and she seemed to understand. He told Theresa that we were supposed to have a fight. The director told him to tell her that she had to let my feet come up, because it would look funny. Once again, we talked our way through it but didn't want to take away the spontaneity of the moment by overrehearsing. Well, the time came for us to get in the vat, which was full of real grapes, and God, it was like stepping on eyeballs. We started stomping on the grapes, and I made a dance out of it, and then I slipped. I didn't mean to, but I did. As I slipped, I accidentally hit Theresa, who took offense, and she hauled off and let me have it. Right in *la banza*. Took all the wind right out of me. Down I went, with Theresa on top of me. My head was supposed to pop up and then my arm and then my leg, and nothing popped up. She just held me down, hitting me. I thought she was trying to kill me. I had grapes up my nose, up my ears. She was choking me. The audience thought it was part of the show, and they were hysterical. I started beating her back to get her off of me. Finally, I gave her one good shove and threw her off and yelled, 'Cut!' I had to catch my breath. The director came over and calmed Theresa down and then calmed me down, and said we had to continue with the fight. The translator came over and explained it all again, and I thought it was okay. As soon as he yelled, 'Action,' the fight was on again. I thought it was my last moments on earth."

Lucy almost called for a "cut" because of the intense pain she was having during the filming of another episode, one called *The Passports*. When Lucy can't find her birth certificate (without which she won't be able to get a passport and go to Europe), she wonders if she could fit into Fred's steamer trunk and go as a stowaway.

Lucy gets in the trunk to "try it on for size" when she is accidentally locked in. She has to stay there until Fred finds the lost key. Lucy had to stay in the trunk for over five minutes on her knees. During the filming, she was overcome with claustrophobia. As the scene progressed, her legs ached more and more until the pain was almost unbearable.

Late in the scene, Ricky uses the trunk as a conga drum and as he began pounding, Lucy thought it was over for her. Between the lack of air and the pain in her legs, Lucy thought she would faint and almost called for a cut. Instead, she put her mouth on the air hole, took several deep breaths, and went on. When she finally got out of the trunk, her moans and groans as she straightens up weren't good acting. She hurt.

Lucy told John another story as she put the William Holden episode of *I Love Lucy* into the VCR. She told him she had another close call. "Bill was a friend, and we asked him to do it. Big stars weren't doing guest appearances at the time, but he read the script and said yes right away. In the scene where I don't want him to recognize me because I dumped a whole plate of spaghetti on him, I wore a long nose, which kept getting longer every time I scratched it. In rehearsal, Bill lit my cigarette and nothing happened which was not supposed to happen. At the filming, he lit my cigarette and

149

my nose went up in flames. I blew it out, keeping in character, and all I could think of was to dip the end of it into a cup of coffee. You can see Desi and Bill trying not to break up."

During the same season, Lucy in Hollywood decided to fool her nearsighted friend Carolyn into thinking she is a cavalcade of famous movie stars, including Jimmy Durante and Clark Gable. Meanwhile, Ricky runs into Harpo Marx and asks him to drop by to say hello, just as Lucy herself is posing as Harpo. They recreated the mirror scene from *Duck Soup*, with Lucy pretending to be Harpo's mirror image.

"Harpo was such a darling man. Bright and witty and articulate for someone who never spoke on-camera, but when he worked, he always worked alone. If you look back at the Marx Brothers films, you'll see Groucho and Chico working together, with Harpo doing his own thing in and out of the picture. I was supposed to imitate everything he did, but he couldn't remember from one rehearsal to the next what it was he did. We went crazy. It ended up that I had to teach him his own routine. He was a great musician and a great guy."

Lucy liked to work with her friends. "I

feel comfortable having people I know around. That's why they kept popping up playing different things on different weeks." One of those friends included Mary Wickes. "We hired 'Sister Wickes' to play my ballet teacher. Mary and I liked to surprise each other, so we didn't rehearse ourselves to death. She used the phrase 'A bas!' I didn't know what it meant, but I thought it was funny, so I kept saying, 'A bas! A bas!' all the way through the scene. Then I got my foot caught on the barre and almost broke my leg. If it had been another inch down, it would have snapped. Then I really would have yelled, *'A bas!'* "

Lucy made sure that Bea Benaderet and Gale Gordon both worked on the show, even though they couldn't be regulars. Gale Gordon played Mr. Littlefield, the owner of the Tropicana nightclub in several episodes, and Bea Benaderet played Mrs. Lewis, one of the Ricardos' neighbors, who was in love with the local butcher (another pal, Edward Everett Horton).

"We were friends with Jerry Hausner, who played Ricky's agent," Lucy said. "He also played the stage manager in the 'Vita-meta-vegamin' sequence. I just stare at him like a drunken sot. That was such fun to do.

I loved playing a drunk. I almost got sick to my stomach after that show. There was pure honey in that bottle. Try drinking honey straight and see how *you* like it."

When Lucy finished the "Vita-meta-vegamin" cassette, she asked the little boy what he wanted to watch next. He asked Lucy which one she enjoyed the most. She told him the one she had the most fun doing. "I love the episode about 'The Pleasant Peasant.' We tried to do different things every week, and we knew Viv could sing and I couldn't. I played the old Gypsy who crawls out of the well, remember?"

John shook his head yes.

"Everybody thinks that I'm acting when I try to find my note, but that's not acting. I couldn't find my note if you handed it to me."

Lucy was outspoken about the episodes she thought were less than successful. "That Christmas show is terrible. I'm glad they never show it." The show she was referring to was a Christmas Eve show in which Fred buys a tree and Lucy has him trim off the branches that ruin the line. Of course, by the time he's finished, there is only the bare tree trunk left. As Lucy gives Fred his tree-trimming instructions, they flash back to previous episodes, including Lucy telling Ricky she's pregnant, the birth of Little Ricky, and the barbershop quartet. The show has an almost metaphysical ending, where the "real" Santa Claus is discovered in the Ricardo kitchen and slowly fades into thin air. I watched the Christmas show with Lucy, and it *was* strange. It seemed as if they were Lucy and Desi instead of "Lucy" and Ricky. Several times during the show, Lucy is out of character, breaking concentration, looking offstage. The show was pulled from the syndication package, and has only been seen a few times since 1957.

One of Lucy's least-favorite shows featured a guest appearance by Orson Welles. When Lucy hears that Orson needs an assistant for an appearance at Ricky's club, she volunteers for the job (what else?) thinking that Orson needs a Juliet to play opposite his Romeo. What Orson wants is a girl to levitate as part of his nightclub magic act.

Lucy spoke fondly of Orson, even though he drove her crazy. "People say *I'm* difficult to work with? Well, you should have seen Orson. We wanted him on the show to give him something to do, since he was living in our guest house and was eating us out of house and home. But that's another story.

Orson had this trick where I was being levitated on the end of the broom, and it was the most painful experience of my life. Worse than childbirth. It felt like the broom was up my ass, and I had to stay on the goddamned thing for at least five minutes. Orson wanted to wear tails in the scene, but he wouldn't go for a fitting. Elois Jensen, who did all the clothes, got the biggest tails she could find. They were like big velour drapes that you used for backdrops, and Orson put them on at the dress rehearsal. It was like putting skin on a sausage. He put me on the broom for the dress rehearsal, and made some sweeping gesture and rrrrip! The tails split right up the back. There was no time to get another set. Another set of tails didn't exist that could get around him, so Elois cut some black cloth and pinned it the best she could. If you look at the show, you'll see how self-conscious he is about turning his back to the audience. God, that show was a stinker."

Little John laughed when Lucy called the show a stinker. He said to her, "You're funny." She said, "Thank you." The boy and his parents stayed with Lucy for a couple of hours. He asked if he could have his picture taken with her, and she said yes. Then she brought out her own instant camera and asked if she could have *her* picture taken with him. His ashen face lit up. They posed for several pictures together, and then the family left.

The limousine at the end of the walkway had attracted a lot of attention, and a small crowd had gathered to see if Lucy would come out. She opened the front door, and they began to applaud, click off several pictures and yell to her. John and his parents started down the walk. About halfway, he turned around, leaving his parents, and walked back to Lucy, who was still standing at the front door. He looked up at her and softly said to her, "Would you please pray for me?"

Lucy took him in her arms and hugged him. "I already have, John. Pray for me, too?" She kissed him on the cheek, waited for him to get in the car, and closed the door. When she turned to me, tears were rolling down her cheeks. I took her in my arms and held her while she sobbed. She looked at me and said, "And we think we have problems."

CHAPTER
Eleven

LUCY INVITED ME to a black-tie dinner on March 11, 1989, where Lucie Arnaz was performing. It was a benefit for the Valley Presbyterian Hospital, one of Lucy's favorite charities. She looked forward to the event, and kept kidding me about how I'd look in a tuxedo. I told her I looked like Orson Welles playing a maître d' at McDonald's.

The dinner and show was held in the lobby of the MGM Film Center, a ten-story glass atrium that had been transformed into an elegant supper club. Lucy and Gary invited me; Audrey Meadows; producer Ray Katz; Lucy's publicist, Tom Watson; songwriter Steve Schalchlin; Lucy's friend from New York Lee Tannen; her secretary, Wanda Clark, with her husband, Peter Stomatovich; Paula Stewart; and Gary's sister, Helen.

Lucy was in a festive mood along with everyone else. We all played musical chairs so we could visit with each other and laugh. When Lucie's show started, I ended up sitting between Lucy and Audrey Meadows.

Lucie, backed up by two boys and a

twelve-piece orchestra, performed a program of Irving Berlin. It was a great show. Lucie introduced her mother, and the applause thundered and echoed off the high glass walls. I helped Lucy out of her chair, and experienced something almost metaphysical when the bright white spotlight hit her face. As she was absorbed in the light, it took thirty years off of her and infused her with energy. She was Lucy in her prime again. She turned, bowed, and blew kisses to the crowd. She loved every minute of it.

After the show, we went backstage to say hi to Lucie. There is nothing more exciting in the world than to be in the star's dressing room after a great performance. A guard at the door saw Steve Schalchlin holding a camera and told him he wasn't allowed to take pictures backstage. When Lucy embraced her daughter, I grabbed the camera from him and took a picture of them hugging. To my knowledge, it's the last photo of them taken together.

As we left the hall, people were lined up to talk to Lucy and get her autograph. They wanted to touch her or speak to her or just be near her. She made people happy with her presence. One of the ladies in the group told her that she would never forget the night that Little Ricky was born. Another lady echoed her. "Desi was in that witch-doctor mask." Another lady jumped in, "And they almost left you behind." They all had their own memories of that show; the night that almost everyone in America was watching *I Love Lucy*.

Lucy talked to the ladies as if they were old friends over for coffee. She talked about the show, and told them about trying to get pregnant in real life. Lucy said, "Desi and I agreed to do a command performance for Queen Elizabeth—the Second, not the First. We had been asked a few years before to do it, said yes, and then found out we were going to have Lucie. So, a few days after we accepted the second time, I found out I was pregnant again. I told Desi we could've had children years before, if we had only agreed to a command performance."

The ladies laughed. In the middle of 1952, when Lucy found out she was going to have another baby, nobody was laughing, especially CBS. They flatly refused to let Lucy appear on the air "with child." They told Desi that if they agreed to continue the show at all, she would have to be photographed behind couches or partitions to cover her bulging tummy. Also, no mention of the pregnancy would be allowed.

Desi knew that Lucy couldn't do the same kind of physical shows they had been doing with a child on the way. He wanted to address the issue directly and incorporate the birth into the story line of the show. Again the network refused. Desi stood firm. He got very dramatic and told them it would be the end of the number-one television show if they didn't agree.

Desi knew the ultimate power did not rest with the network, it rested with the sponsor of the show. He went to Arthur Lyons, chairman of the board of Philip Morris, and asked him to make the final decision. Desi explained that the show was top-rated because he was calling the creative shots. If he couldn't call the shots anymore, then he did not want to be held responsible when the show fell in the ratings. Lyons agreed to let Desi do what he thought was right and sent a memo to Jim Aubrey, chairman of CBS. The memo was to the point: "Dear Jim, Don't fuck around with the Cuban. Arthur."

Lucy remembered those days vividly. "It was like walking on eggshells. We could incorporate the birth into the show, but we could never use the word 'pregnant'. Isn't that funny? We couldn't use the word, and today they show you how to get in the condition. We had a priest, a minister, and a rabbi. It looked like a revival meeting around the place. They all thought the scripts were in very good taste, which they were. All we did was put in some of the things that happened to us and every other couple that's expecting. They couldn't object to that. The first show we did about it, when I tell Ricky I'm pregnant, was something to go through. You would have thought we were doing *Medea* with all the crying around the place. But we got through it. Those were terrific shows."

Once they had the go-ahead from CBS to include the pregnancy in the story, they had to make a decision as to whether the Ricardo child would be a boy or girl. Lucy said, "I remember all the hoopla that was made about it, but there was never any doubt that the baby on the show would be a boy, and for one reason and one reason alone. We had a very precocious two-year-old girl on our hands, and if the Ricardo baby was a girl, then Lucie would never understand why it wasn't her. It was just best for everybody that it was a boy."

January 19, 1953, was the night the Ricardo baby was born. On the same morning, Lucy delivered Desiderio Alberto Arnaz y de Acha IV by cesarean section. Lucy remembered the day and said, "Everyone was patting themselves on the back that it was a boy. As if I had nothing to do with it." More people watched the birth of Little Ricky than the inauguration of Dwight Eisenhower as president the next day.

Desi had made a deal with *TV Guide* that it would get the first pictures of the Arnaz baby. "Desi was very sharp about such things," Lucy said. "*TV Guide* hounded him for months about getting the baby's picture first, and Desi told them that if they wanted it, they would have to pay for it. I have no idea what he made the deal for, but he did and it was set. A few weeks after Desi was born, we had a fellow from another magazine out to the house for an interview. Desi offered him a drink, and the two of them hit it off, and I think they even played cards. Anyway, Desi showed him the pictures that he had promised *TV Guide*. He felt bad. He liked the guy from the competition so much that he wanted to give him the pictures first, but couldn't because of his exclusive contract with the other magazine. After a few more drinks, Desi looked at the guy and said, 'I'm going to leave the room for a few minutes, but I'm going to leave the pictures here. *You better not take one picture and put it in your pocket before you go.'* When the picture showed up in the other magazine before it turned up in *TV Guide,* there was nothing they could do about it. The picture was stolen."

During the third season of *I Love Lucy,* Desi came home in an uproar. "I was home taking care of the baby, and Desi came in with three or four cardboard boxes of papers. He was fuming and yelling in Spanish like he would on the show, "Miraquegueroco-sastupido . . ." I asked him what happened, and he said that CBS had accused him of stealing a million dollars. They had gone over the books, and presented him with the million-dollar deficit and told him that he would have to repay it. He moved every piece of furniture out of the living room, and started putting the papers out on the floor. It was about nine-thirty at night, and he asked me to help him. He started spreading all these papers all over the floor, and after a while I got tired. I had to go to work the next day early, and so I went to bed. When I got up the next morning, Desi wasn't in bed. I went to the living room, and he was still on the floor with all the papers all over the place. Wall-to-wall. He said, "I found it." We went to CBS the next day, and into the guy's office who said Desi had lost the money. Desi asked him for a rehearsal studio so he could show him the mistake. The guy was very snotty to him, and said it couldn't be arranged. Desi blew his top and said, 'Then everybody will have to know what an asshole you are!' He went out into the corridor and started putting the papers down end-to-end. They went down one whole hallway, made a turn, and down another hallway. Secretaries, office boys, executives . . . everybody was at their doors watching as Desi led the asshole down the corridor paper by paper. Desi proved the guy wrong. He showed him exactly where the mistakes were made. They never fooled around with him after that."

Lucy was finally enjoying the adulation and superstardom she had worked so hard for. By the midfifties, the girl from Celoron, New York, was one of the most famous women in the world. Lucy found it had a price. "I was always so open to people, but I started to find that some people wanted to be my friend not for my friendship, but for what they could get out of it. For instance,

I knew Hedda Hopper well enough to say hello and chat at a party, but all of a sudden, she'd stop by the house while she was walking her dogs and ring the bell. I always let her in, but I was very guarded about what I would say to her. It got to the point where I dreaded seeing her. One day she rang the bell and came right in as usual. I was sitting in the den, and I was startled to see her. Hedda never pulled her punches. She said, 'You're afraid of me, aren't you?' I tried to act my way out of it. 'Hedda, why should I be afraid of you?'

"You have no reason to be, but you are. Am I right or wrong?' she said.

"I told her she was right. I told her that I didn't want everything that ever happened in my house to appear in her column. I thought she was a nice lady, but I didn't trust her. She took my hand and said, 'Lucille, you can trust me.' She told me she really liked me and wanted my friendship. We were two dames in a town full of sharks, and we could help each other. From that moment on, I felt we really were friends. She helped me so much over the years. More than the mayor, more than the police department, more than the chamber of commerce, I felt that Hedda ran Hollywood.

Whenever she wanted something done, it was done. So many times, Desi would get thrown out of some bordello and the police would throw him on the front lawn and then ring the bell. They'd say, 'Here's your husband, lady,' and then leave. He was absolutely passed out. I'd try and drag him up the steps, but I couldn't move him. Within a few minutes, without my calling her, Hedda would appear on my doorstep and help me get him inside. I guess there was somebody on the police force who tipped her off to all the dirt; and believe me, Desi was dirt. She could have used all that stuff about his affairs. He was never very discreet, but she wouldn't. She always kept it out of other peoples columns, too. One day she came over. By this time, I'd look forward to her little visits. Besides Vivian, she was my best girlfriend. This one day she came over, and I knew something was wrong. She said she didn't want to talk about it. I told her that trust was a two-way street. If she wanted me to trust her, then she would have to trust me. She cried. It was her son, William. His marriage was ending."

William Hopper was a dashing man in his mid-forties, with a classic profile and a shock of white hair. He was then playing the part of Paul Drake, Perry Mason's private investigator, on Raymond Burr's top-rated television show.

"Hedda finally came out with it. Bill had two children, and his marriage was on the rocks because he had fallen in love with one of the biggest stars on television at the time. It was a man. You never used the word 'gay' back then. He was 'queer' or a 'fag' or a 'fairy,' but never 'gay.' I couldn't believe who it was when she told me, because you don't think about this guy as being anything but straight. I won't tell you who it is, because he's still one of the biggest stars on TV. Anyway, it broke Hedda's heart. The fellow loved Bill very much, and I understand their relationship lasted until Bill died. It was very sad."

Lucy thought about how Hedda would urge her to give parties. Hedda would flit around the room picking up dirt like a human vacuum cleaner. Lucy looked around the room and thought out loud about good times she had there. "We were very social at that time. We loved to go to parties and have people in, but Desi would always get drunk, and I always got embarrassed. One night we went to Bill Holden's for dinner, and it was fun at first, but we couldn't eat until two of the other guests arrived, and they were almost an hour late. The tardy two were Ron and Nancy Reagan. Desi had time for a few extra cocktails, and was sailing by the time the Reagans arrived. They were all out of breath and so excited and said they couldn't help being late because of what happened. Are you ready? They saw a UFO and stopped to watch it. After he was elected president, I kept thinking about that night, and wondered if he'd have still won if he told everybody that he'd seen a flying saucer."

Lucy told a story about another Hollywood legend—one of TV's most enduring stars. "She and I were doing a public-service commercial for something at a studio, and I had my clothes with me to change for an affair I had to go to that night. I was going to check into a hotel so that I wouldn't have to drive back to Northridge. I got on the phone calling around town to see if there were any rooms I could check into for an hour or so, and this lady overheard what I was saying. She invited me back to her house, and said I could use one of the bedrooms there. I accepted. I followed her back to the house, and we went in. It was a great place. She was going to her suite to take a shower, and asked me if I wanted a drink.

I told her I didn't, but I asked her if she minded if I smoked. She said no, and told me there were cigarettes on the coffee table and I should help myself. I thanked her but said I had my own brand. Well, she went off to take a shower, and I reached into my purse for my cigarettes and I didn't have any. I went over to the coffee table and opened one of the cigarette boxes, and it was full of the most beautiful cigarettes I had ever seen in my life. They were all pastel colors—some were blue, some pink, but they were all trimmed in gold leaf. I lit one and took a couple of puffs and thought they tasted funny. Tasty but funny. I took another drag and another, and in a few minutes the room was going around. I looked at my eyes in the mirror, and my pupils seemed bigger than my head. I finished the cigarette though, and then, and don't ask me why, I had another one. Boy, that was something. The star came back about twenty minutes later, and was surprised that I was still sitting in the living room, staring into space. I told her I loved her cigarettes. She looked at me funny (I *think* she looked funny) and asked me what cigarettes I smoked. I pointed to the box and asked her why they tasted so good. She looked very surprised. She said they were

168

menthol. She had them imported from Turkey. Menthol cigarettes became popular a few years later and, boy, those menthols didn't taste anything like them."

As we were talking, the phone rang. It was Sheila MacRae. Lucy asked Frank to tell Sheila she was taking a nap. Frank came back and said that Sheila wanted to know if she could "hitch a ride" with Gary and her to Milton Berle's eightieth birthday party. Lucy said it would be all right with her. She looked at the calendar to see when the birthday party was, and kept turning page after page. Finally, she found Milton's birthday on a certain page and said, "Hitch a ride? Is she crazy? Milton Berle's birthday isn't for three months. What is she asking for a ride now for?" (When the time came for Milton's party, Sheila found her own transportation.)

When Sheila called, I was reminded of the *I Love Lucy* show that featured the wives of movie stars modeling Don Loper dresses in a celebrity fashion show. "We used all our friends. Sheila. Ardis Holden. It was fun except for one wife who showed up stoned, and stayed that way. When she came down the ramp, we all held our breath that she didn't fall over. I understood it. Hollywood women can turn to drink. It's a wonder I never turned into a boozer myself."

Lucy told me about a big surprise she got one day when she got home. "I walked in the door and came into the den, and I jumped. There was this big fat woman sitting in that chair. [She pointed to a green armchair that's in the doorway between the lanai and the dining room.] The lady looked up at me and said, 'Hello!' I looked at her and said, 'Hello,' and then looked around for help. I had a Chinese couple at the time, who let the woman in. She told them she was a friend of mine and was waiting for a cab. She went to the liquor cabinet, and poured herself a big glass of gin. I could tell she'd had a lot to drink, and so I wasn't about to offer her another one. She looked up at me and said, 'You don't recognize me, do you?'

" 'No, I don't. Have we met?'

"She got a little snarly. 'Of course we've met. Now that you're Miss Television, you don't remember your old friends.'

"I kept looking at her. She was so bloated, I didn't know. I was at a loss. I didn't know if she was a crazy lady or what, and so I said, 'What's your name?'

" 'I'm Yvonne DeCarlo!'

"As soon as she said that, I realized it *was* Yvonne DeCarlo. I remembered the last time I had met her, and in fact, the *only* time I met her. It was 1946, and we were at a makeup room over at Columbia. She came in and sat down next to me and said, 'I've just been voted the most beautiful woman in the world.' I said, 'How nice for you,' and that was the end of it. That was the only time we'd ever met. A few minutes later, her cab arrived and she left. She looked at me and said, 'Thanks for the hospitality!,' got in the cab, and drove off."

Lucy and I stopped playing long enough to watch the news of George Bush's election. It was only about six o'clock in California when the networks projected him as the winner. I said to her, very lightheartedly, "Did you go out and do your civic duty today?"

She got serious. "What do you mean?"

"Did you vote?"

"No! I didn't vote," she said emphatically. "I haven't voted since they called me a communist. And I won't. Let's play."

CHAPTER
Twelve

"IT WAS THE worst week of my life." Lucy didn't like to talk about the days she was called a Communist. Thirty years later, it still pained. her. The voter registration form she marked "Communist" to please her grandfather turned up in front of one of the investigating subcommittees of the House Un-American Activities Committee. A year before Desi, Jr., was born, they asked her why she became a Communist?

"It sounded so silly for a grown-up woman to say, 'I did it because my grandpa wanted me to.' He thought I was a complete idiot or a liar, but he didn't know Daddy. I told you he was nuts. I told you about the scenes about workers' rights and unions and God knows what. Harriet quit at least three times because Daddy told her slavery was dead and that she was better than being a maid to some actress. It always worked out for Harriet, because after one of his tirades, she always got a big raise to make her stay. Daddy just wanted everybody to be treated fairly, that's all. I told all that to the man from the committee, and I thought that was the end of it. I *hoped* it was the end of it. I saw so many careers go right down the drain. I could see mine going along with them."

Almost a year passed before she heard from the committee again. They asked her to come to the office and clear up a few things. Lucy complied. She and Desi answered questions about the Communist registration, meetings in her home, a subscription to *The Daily Worker*, and why she was listed as a delegate to a Communist convention. Lucy answered everything to the man's satisfaction, and he told them that was "the end of it." It was only the beginning.

The week of hell began on Sunday evening, September 6, 1953. Lucy remembered, "I was starting to believe that it was all right. We were about to go into the third season. I thought if they were going to do anything, they would have done it. I was in Northridge, sitting in a rocker like an old lady knitting. I can picture it as if it were yesterday. The radio was on, and I was listening to Walter Winchell. He said, 'What famous redheaded comedienne is a card-carrying communist?' My mouth dropped opened. I tried to guess. Honest to God, I didn't know who he was talking about. My first thought was Eve Arden. Then I thought it couldn't be Eve. Then I thought it was Gracie Allen. Then I thought it was Joan Davis, except she was blond. I never thought it was me. A few minutes later, the phone rang. It was Desi. He was down in Del Mar, where we had a little place, and said, 'Are you all right?'

"'Sure. Why shouldn't I be all right?'

"'Didn't you hear Winchell?'

"'Yeah, I heard him. What about it?'

"'He was talking about you. Don't panic. I'm on my way.'

"When he hung up, I just started crying. It must have been three hours before he got home. It seemed like five. I cried until he got there. Hedda called. She had heard the Winchell thing, too. I didn't know what to tell her. I lied. I said I didn't know what they were talking about. Hedda could have turned on me, but she didn't. She stayed loyal."

Lucy thought that the blind item Winchell spoke of in his broadcast might remain just that. She wanted to keep quiet about the whole thing to see if it would blow over. Desi thought they should confront the situation openly. The choice was taken away the next

174

day when a newspaper headline announced,
LUCILLE BALL A RED

"I saw everything going down the toilet, and I saw so many people going down with us. If we were thrown off the air, then everybody was thrown off with us. We were doing Eve Arden in *Our Miss Brooks* with Gale, and that would have been canceled. Eve was a friend, and I didn't want anything to happen to her. She called me and told me I had her full support. We were friends in 1936, and she knew Daddy drove us all crazy and I wasn't a communist. I woke up the next day (not as though I slept), and I pulled up the blind and the lawn was covered with reporters. Desi went wild. He was on them, pushing them, screaming at them. His Latin blood was at overboil. He kept screaming, 'My wife is not a commie! My wife is not a commie!' Jesus. What a way to start a day."

The newspapers reprinted the testimony that Lucy had given the week before. She summed up the story in her final statement:

I am very happy to have this opportunity to discuss all the things that have cropped up, that apparently I have done wrong. I am aware of only one thing that was wrong and at the time it wasn't wrong, but apparently it is now, and that was registering because my grandfather wanted us to. I at no time thought it was the thing to do, nor did I ever intend to vote in the Presidential election . . . I didn't vote, but I did register. Since then I have never knowingly done anything against the United States. I have never done anything for the Communists, to my knowledge, at any time. I have never contributed money or attended a meeting or ever had anything to do with people connected with it, if to my knowledge they were. I am not a Communist now. I have never been. I never wanted to be. Nothing in the world could ever change my mind. At no time in my life have I ever been in sympathy with anything that even faintly resembled it . . . It sounds a little weak and silly and corny now but at the time it was very important because we knew we weren't going to have Daddy with us for very long. If it made him happy, it was important at the time. But I was always conscious of the fact that I could only go just so far to make him happy. I tried not to go any further. In those days, that was not a big terrible thing to do. It was almost as terrible to be a Republican in those days. I

Lucy in the Afternoon

You can see by this photo how hard it was to make Lucille laugh. Just before this was taken, I whispered in her ear, "Dukakis!"

Audrey Meadows and I are wondering if Lucy will like the lemonade.

I took this picture of Lucy and Lucie over a security guard's objections backstage at the Filmland Center on March 11, 1989, six weeks before Lucy's death. This is one of the last pictures of mother and daughter together.

Lucy showing me how to pull up a chair without breaking it .

Desi, Jr., is as easy to make laugh as his mother.

Lucy's last autograph.

have certainly never been too civic minded and certainly never political minded in my life.

The committee thanked her for her co-operation.

As I read the testimony, I thought about an incident in which Lucy had to sign some papers. When Gary and I made the deal to turn my play *The Lucky O'Learys* into a television series, it was to be a joint venture between Lucille Ball Productions and Twentieth Century-Fox. Gary brought the contracts home for Lucy and me to sign, and she never read a word on the contract when she put her signature to it. She trusted Gary implicitly. I could see her doing the same thing when her grandfather gave her Communist-registration papers to sign. If she trusted the person who was asking her to sign something, that was good enough for her.

Lucy was still shook up by the incident thirty years later, when she talked about what happened the rest of that horrible September week. "Hedda called me again after the shit hit the fan. She was furious that I had lied to her, and I thought, There goes the ball game. I thought I had lost her support, and if Hedda turned against me, it would have been the same as the Supreme Court taking away my citizenship. But she understood. She told me that she was my friend for life."

Hedda didn't believe the newspaper accounts that painted Lucy as a militant pinko activist who would do everything she could do to help subvert America. She didn't like Winchell, and she never spoke to him again for breaking the story. "Hedda took a lot of heat for publicly supporting me," Lucy said. "They accused *her* of being a commie because she took my side. What a circus that was. You know what's funny? I even heard somebody call Mrs. Roosevelt a commie once, and she was the most American American who ever lived."

The three-ring circus found the Arnazes in the center ring, the press in the second ring, and CBS in the third. A network naturally eschews any hint of scandal, knowing that it will hit them right in the pocketbook. CBS's biggest star was being faced with her signed membership registration in the Communist party. They had to make a decision before the show went back into production. Do they keep an accused Communist on in a comedy when the preceding news show is filled with Senator Joseph McCarthy playing out his tragedy?

Frank Stanton, then president of the network, had two choices. He could listen to the columnists who were telling him to take her off the air and burn her at the stake, or to Desi, who told him they would totally clear Lucy and to give them a chance. Stanton bet on Desi.

They plunged into rehearsals for the first show of the third season. I asked Lucy what the episode was, and she shook her head. "I have no idea. All I know is how much I cried." She remembered getting to the studio. "It was like running a gauntlet. I don't know whether those people were shouting that they loved me or they hated me. It was just a roar. I've never cried so much in my life. I'd say a line and cry. I'd have lunch and cry. I'd go home and cry. Then I knew I had to face an audience that thought I was a communist, and I didn't know what they were going to do. I had a dream that they were coming over the barricades with clubs, and they'd beat me to death. I didn't want to do the show that week. Desi said we had to. If we didn't, it would make everybody think we had something to hide. You know, my grandfather had been dead for ten years, but I wished he was alive so I could KILL HIM!''

A few hours before the show was to be filmed, Desi talked to members of the committee, who told him they had absolutely nothing on Lucy, and she would be totally cleared publicly in the morning. As the audience filed in and the cast assembled, waiting for the explosion, Desi was the only one who knew that the bomb had been defused. He was anxious to share the news.

Along with introducing so many original techniques to the art of TV, Desi also gave us the audience "warm-up." People usually stood on line for up to an hour before being let into a studio, and their mood was not always receptive to comedy. Desi would come out before the show and do a number with the orchestra and tell a few jokes so they could get a sound level. They wanted the laughs recorded, but not the customary entrance applause that greeted star performers. So Desi would introduce the cast first, and the show would begin.

The audience was in place on Friday night, September 11, and when Desi appeared, the spectators became intensely quiet. They had become part of the biggest news story in America. There would be no jokes during this warm-up. Desi himself recalled the moment in his memoir, *A Book*.

"I went out front and said, 'Ladies and gentlemen, I know you've read a lot of bad headlines about my wife today. I came from Cuba. My family was thrown out of Cuba because we fought the Communists. We hated them. They destroyed our lives and I wasn't about to marry one. During my years in the United States Army I became an American citizen, and one of the things I admire about this country is that you're innocent until proven guilty. Up to now, you've only read what people have said about Lucy, but you have not had a chance to read our answer to those accusations. I assure you that the only thing red about my wife is her hair—and even that isn't real! (Big laugh) So I will ask you to do only one thing tonight and that is to reserve your judgment until you read the newspapers tomorrow. In the meantime, I hope you can enjoy the show under these trying circumstances."

Then, as usual, he introduced Bill Frawley and Vivian Vance. The crowd welcomed them enthusiastically. Desi continued, "And now I want you to meet the girl to whom I've been married for the last thirteen years and who I know is as American as J. Edgar

Hoover and Barney Baruch, my favorite wife, the mother of my children, the vice president of Desilu Productions—I am the president —the girl who plays Lucy—Lucille Ball!''

The explosion came in a volley of applause. Loud, sustained, enthusiastic, loving applause. Lucy came out and bowed and wept. She ran up to the bleachers and kissed her mother and her cousin Cleo. She shook as many hands as she could, and returned to the stage. All she could get out were a few tearful thank yous.

Lucy and Desi held a press conference two days later at the Desilu ranch. The same reporters who were peering into their bedroom a few days before were now there as their guests. The day before, the committee admitted it had nothing on television's most popular star. Lucy and Desi gave the reporters the details. That night, September 12, a week after he started the whole mess, Walter Winchell announced that ''Donald Jackson, chairman of the House Un-American Activities Committee, and all its members cleared Lucy a hundred percent, and so did J. Edgar Hoover and the FBI, plus every newspaper in America, and tonight Mr. Lincoln [using him as a metaphor for America] is drying his tears for making her go through this.''

Lucy laughed when I read this to her, and said, "Lincoln didn't make me go through it, Winchell did!"

CHAPTER
Thirteen

ONE AFTERNOON, I had an appointment in Beverly Hills not far from Lucy's house. The meeting finished much earlier than I expected, so I drove over to Lucy's. I was about an hour earlier than usual, but I knew she wouldn't mind if we spent more time together. She took a shower about 11:00 A.M., had something light to eat, and then read until I got there. When I walked in, she was in the lanai reading. I caught her by surprise. She hadn't yet put on her makeup. I had never seen her without lipstick, and she looked so different. Lucy without her famous bow lips.

"Hi! Did you finish already?" she said.

"I did. Are you ready for some fast action?"

"Not without makeup." She got out of her chair and went to the backgammon table, where she kept a small makeup bag.

"Are you going to be funny today?" she

asked me as she looked into her compact mirror.

"Absolutely. I'm going to be a laugh riot."

"Good. Then I won't put on any mascara."

She took a tube of pink lipstick and swabbed her lips quickly. Suddenly, she was Lucy again. She dabbed her lips with a tissue, handed it to me, and said, "Throw that in the wastepaper basket, will you?"

Putting the tissue in my shirt pocket, I said, "Are you kidding? I can get ten dollars apiece for these."

Lucy laughed and reached again for the tube of lipstick. "Well, if you get ten dollars apiece, you might as well get a good one." She redid her lips, this time very meticulously, and blotted them on one of the initialed cocktail napkins on the table. She handed me the napkin with a perfect outline of the famous lips. "Maybe you can get twenty-five for that!" I didn't even try. I took the lip prints home and framed them.

Gary came in a few minutes later. Lucy didn't get up to kiss him as she usually did. Her attitude was mock icy.

"I called you at the club. They said you weren't there. What's her name?"

Gary smiled. "Her name is the sand trap

on the fifteenth hole." Lucy jumped up and put her arms around him. "Well, that's all right then." They kissed for a long time. Gary went into the kitchen to have his coffee, and Lucy sat down again. She was never jealous of Gary. She knew that when Gary was out in the afternoon, the only other person in his life was his caddie. When Gary left the room, she said, "It's not like with the other one. If he was gone in the afternoon, I always knew where he was, except I didn't *want* to know. Desi had a place up in the Hollywood Hills that he thought nobody knew about. *Everybody* knew about it. Once Desi got a call here from somebody who was looking for him, so I gave him Desi's number at his 'shack-up' place. I told the guy to try him there. He was there. The guy found him, I know he did, but Desi never said a word about it. That was part of the Latin mentality—if you don't talk about it, then it doesn't exist."

In the last year of her life, Lucy had been married to Gary almost ten years longer than she had to Desi. She might have kidded Gary about not being able to find him at the club, but she never doubted his fidelity. "He goes to Palm Springs by himself and he goes on golf tours, and I know that's exactly what he's doing. He calls me to say hello from wherever he is, and I didn't tell him to. He wants to. Desi was just the opposite. He would tell me he was going to business meetings and working lunches, and I knew that was exactly what he *wasn't* doing. You can't change a person, and it's foolish to try."

The more successful the Arnazes were, the more their marriage failed. The happiest times were working together, when they actually said nice things to each other because that was what was written.

With Lucy's communist scandal behind her, MGM decided to go ahead with plans to star Lucy and Desi in *The Long, Long Trailer*. Lucy looked forward to being directed by an old friend, Vincente Minnelli —the ex-husband of Judy Garland and the father of Liza. Lucy was hungry for good directors. She longed for someone to take her firmly in hand and guide her. Most of her directors were terrified of her.

Lucy said to me once, "If any director says to you, 'What do you feel like doing in this scene?,' then run for your life. That's all I ever got."

Minnelli was a strong director, but not at the beginning of the film. Lucy thought about the first day of shooting. She was in her midforties and feared the audience would not accept her as a young newlywed. She needed encouragement and went to Minnelli, who was, according to Lucy, "a basket case."

Lucy defended him. "He was a *great* director. It was Judy who was making him crazy. Judy made *everybody* crazy. They were already divorced, but Judy was going through one of her crazy times. God, that woman was impossible. He [Vincente] was trying to take care of Liza, and Judy wanted her, but Judy was so drunk and so full of pills that he didn't want Liza to be with her. Jesus, it was a mess. So *I* took her."

"What do you mean, you *took* her?"

Lucy looked at me, exasperated. "I mean I took her. I didn't steal her, if that's what you mean. Vincente didn't think Liza should be with her grandparents, and he knew that Judy was in no condition to raise her, so I said I'd take her. We had two kids who were a little younger than Liza, but I told him that if I could take care of two, then I could take care of three. He grabbed my hand and just kept saying, 'Will you? Will you?' Liza was with us for almost a year. She's a good kid. Wild but good. Judy wasn't a good mother. To this day, I can't stand listening to her voice." (This was confirmed a few weeks later, when we were listening to a tape that designer Don Feld had given Lucy—a collection of hit songs from MGM. "We're a Couple of Swells" started playing, and Lucy looked up with a scowl on her face. "Is that Judy?" I told her it was. She yelled as if her hand were caught in a hot fire, "Take her off! Take her off!")

The Long, Long Trailer was a big hit. The public didn't care if Lucy and Desi played newlyweds or deaf Eskimos, it wanted to see them.

Lucy was still having fun doing the "Lucy" character. She said, "My job was easy. All I had to do was act. Desi was doing everything. At first, everybody thought it was me who was calling the shots and making the decisions and coming up with all the ideas, but it wasn't. It was when we started doing other series beside our own and I never showed up at a meeting that they believed that Desi was the brains."

Everyone in the business believed that Desilu meant a quality product. They were a "mom-and-pop studio," hands-on involvement by both of them, and a lot of care went into each show. After only a few years in the business, Desilu Productions was supplying four hours of television a week, including the top-rated *Our Miss Brooks*, *December Bride*, and *Make Room for Daddy*.

"Desi was the idea man," Lucy said, "but he had a couple that really backfired in our faces. Orson Welles was one."

"You mean because of the guest shot he did when he split his tails?" I asked.

Lucy chuckled. "That was only a part of it. I had a real love-hate relationship with Orson." She laughed. "But he had a love-hate relationship with himself, so it was all right."

"Why did you hate him?"

"Because he was so wasteful. He left a huge trail of garbage in his wake. He did it with everything. He left debts behind, wives behind, children behind, everything, as he just sailed through life. Very irresponsible. I ought to know. He lived with us forever."

"When?"

"I have no idea. [I found out it was 1955.] Desi wanted to do an anthology series, you know, a different show every week. He also wanted to work with Orson, who he thought was a great genius—which he was. That's why I loved him. His mind was awesome . . . but he was also a pain in the ass. Anyway, Orson was in Europe doing something because he couldn't get back in the States without being arrested for tax evasion. He was always in trouble with some government because of something. He was living in Italy, and Desi called him and asked him to come and do *The Fountain of Youth* as a pilot for the anthology show. [*The Fountain of Youth* was a story about Ponce de Léon and his search for the mythological waters of eternal spring.] Orson said he'd love to do it, but couldn't come back to America at the moment. Desi understood, and paid off Orson's debts so that the government would let him back in."

"When Orson got to the States, he said he had no place to go. Desi offered to put him up at the Beverly Hills Hotel, but Orson said he didn't think he could be at his best creatively without a family environment. He had left his pregnant wife behind and didn't want to be alone." Lucy threw up her hands and said, "So he moved in with us!"

Lucy and I went for a walk around the property. She loved to take care of the flowers, and was very proud of her gardening. We stopped in front of the guest house and went in. The guest house was one large room divided into a living area and a bedroom area. In one corner was a kitchenette, and in another was a dressing room and bathroom. Pictures of Lucy in her starlet days were everywhere.

"This is where Orson spent ten years."

"Ten years?"

"Well, it was only a few months, but it seemed like ten years. He had the servants hopping. He'd walk in the living room, all in black with his big cigar blowing, and scare the hell out of the kids. I heard Little Desi crying one afternoon, and I thought, Orson's home. He thought this was the Arnaz Hotel or something. Orson must have been a king in a former life, because that's the way he wanted everybody to treat him in this one. He *was* 'The Man Who Came to Dinner.' Desi gave him a budget for *Fountain of Youth,* and sat on him to keep to it. Orson kept futzing and making changes and needing more money and—we put him on the show just to keep him busy before he actually did *Fountain of Youth*—he was spending like a sailor. What's more, he wouldn't let us see what he was doing. It took him months to prepare the thing, and he was supposed to shoot it in a week, but the week turned into a month. Then it was six weeks. Then Orson came to us and he said he needed ten thousand more, and it would be finished in a few days. Desi said yes but warned Orson, 'Dat's dat!' No more money after the ten grand.

"About a week later, Orson asked us over to the stage he was shooting on to see how the extra ten thousand dollars had been spent. We went there expecting to see a scene, or some rushes, or something, and what we got was the biggest wrap party in the history of the world. He'd spent the ten grand on a party! Desi almost punched him in the nose. Orson took the bill out of his pocket and said to Desi,'You can use this as a great business write-off with the IRS.' Desi said to him, 'How would jou know? Jou hafen't paid your taxes in twenty-fife years.' Orson screamed laughing. Got all red in the face. Desi started laughing. We were all holding ourselves. Once Desi and Orson started drinking, that was it. Boy, it was a great party."

Lucy looked around the guest room as she straightened the bedspread. "Orson's wife had a baby while he was living with us, but that still didn't give him any impetus to move. Why should he? He was having a wonderful time out here, living like King Tut."

The Fountain of Youth did not sell the anthology series as Desi had hoped, but it was shown on CBS and won an Emmy—the only unsold pilot ever to have that honor.

The strain on the Arnazes' marriage increased in direct proportion to the growth of their empire. Desi worked all day and made love all night—but not to Lucy.

By 1958, everyone connected with *I Love Lucy* was burning out—including Lucy. She still loved the character, but wasn't having fun anymore. Everyone was fighting. The joy of creating and getting the show to number one was gone. The writers were running out of plots. Vivian Vance was cranky. Bill Frawley was crankier. Desilu was growing into a major force in Hollywood, and Lucy was at the fork in the road.

She told me about the decision she had to make. "Desi wanted to sell everything and retire. Just the word alone sent chills through my body. I loved working. I didn't want to retire ever. I told him that. I felt I didn't have a marriage anymore. Desi wasn't about to give up booze and broads, so I didn't see any reason to give up my work. I wanted to slow down, yes. But I didn't want to stop."

They continued by doing *I Love Lucy* as an hour-long monthly show, *The Lucy-Desi Comedy Hour*. I told Lucy that when I was twelve, I asked my dad about the name change. "How come it's not *I Love Lucy* anymore?" He said he didn't know. I asked him, "Was it because he *doesn't* love Lucy anymore?" Lucy shrugged and said, "I guess so."

Lucy liked doing the hour shows. "I enjoyed them because we got to work with our friends. We had Milton [Berle], and we had Betty Grable and Harry James. You know, Desi had an affair with Betty Grable not long after we were married. I don't think she was married to Harry at the time. Anyway, she was a great gal. If I stayed mad at every woman Desi had an affair with, I'd have been angry with half of the nicest girls in Hollywood."

Lucy wanted to do a show with Bette Davis. "I wanted to work with her since I saw her that day I watched her at Murray Anderson's School. We came up with a great idea. Bette would be renting the house next door to us, and I'd get her involved in a local PTA show. First, she wanted a lot of money, which we gave her, then she wanted a private plane to take her out here from Connecticut or Maine or wherever the hell she lived, and then she wanted this, that, and the other thing. She knew I wanted her, and she knew

I'd give her anything she wanted. So after everything was all set, she went ass over teakettle in her house and broke something, and that was the end of that. We couldn't wait for her to mend, so we had to recast the thing. We went with Tallulah Bankhead, who was impossible. Absolutely impossible. She was loaded most of the time, and she couldn't remember one line to the next, and oh boy! I thought maybe we should call the whole thing off and wait for Bette. We couldn't. I felt sorry for the audience. I thought Tallulah would be so bombed that she'd go up [forget her lines] and curse them all out.

"Well, I went into Tallulah's dressing room before the show to wish her luck, and she was sipping 'coffee.' She mumbled something about 'preparing, dahling!,' and I crossed my fingers. Well, she was perfect. She never missed a cue. She never missed a line. She never missed a laugh. I couldn't get over it. The audience loved her, and it was a very good show."

At the end of the first season, Desi had a call that the RKO Studios was for sale. He had recently bought the Motion Picture Center, but knew that the RKO lot, equipment, and library were a bargain. He got the loan, and the studio that Lucy once worked at as a contract player was now hers.

"It was mind-boggling. I walked around those studio streets that were so full of memories . . . they were mine. Gee!"

After the first season of hour shows, Lucy and Desi were hardly speaking to each other. They were leading separate lives under the same roof. Without the black hair dye, Desi's hair was snow white. He was aging twice as fast, drinking twice as much, and carousing as if there were no tomorrow. Lucy couldn't believe some of Desi's antics. She said, "Sometimes my mother would stay over at the house and bring some friends. We'd put her friends in the guest house. Desi would come home so loaded some nights that I wouldn't let him in the bedroom. I told him he'd have to sleep on the couch. He'd go out to the guest house and try and crawl into bed with my mother's friends. These seventy-year-old women. God, you should have heard the screams.

"I thought if we got away from it all, it might help, so we packed up the kids and went off to Hawaii. Desi couldn't relax, but he sure could drink. That's all he did. He couldn't see straight half the time. Some vacation."

Lucy shifted in her chair and asked me if I wanted to hear something strange. She said about the Hawaiian vacation, "The day before we were supposed to come home, Desi and I had a big fight, and he went swimming out into the ocean and got hit with a wave. He didn't get hurt or anything, but when he came out of the water, his wedding ring, Saint Christopher medal, and the chain that held them came off from around his neck. It was kind of symbolic. Our marriage was gone, why shouldn't his ring be, too?"

The tension between Lucy and Desi during the last season was unbearable. Everyone could feel it. During a break in the filming, Lucy wanted to make one more attempt to save their eighteen-year-old marriage. She suggested that they go to Europe. Lucy showed me the scrapbook of their trip to Capri. Lucy and the kids sightseeing. Lucy and the kids at the ocean. Lucy and the kids dancing with Italian children. "Desi's not in any of the pictures. Where was he?" I asked her.

"That's a good question. He was so out of it, he didn't know if we were in Europe or Pittsburgh. We went to stay with Maurice Chevalier at his home outside of Paris. What a wonderful man he was. He knew we were in a lot of trouble. He told me the end of a love affair is more painful than anything else on earth except for staying in a love affair that had no love left. He was like a father telling me it was all right to let go. We cut the trip short and came back on the *Île-de-France*. It was the last trip for the ship. It was the last trip for all of us."

CHAPTER
Fourteen

A FEW DAYS before the Thanksgiving weekend of 1988, Lucy was feeling blue because she had to go to Palm Springs. She once loved to spend time in the house, but since the stroke, she felt trapped there when Gary was out playing golf—which was most of the day. Gary was reticent about letting her drive alone.

"I wish you could go to Palm Springs for Thanksgiving," she said to me.

"You never let me surprise you," I answered. "I have some friends visiting from New York, and we've rented a condo down the street from you."

She was like a little girl. "Did you really? Are you serious? That's wonderful. God, you made me happy. Do they play backgammon?"

"They're the ones who taught me!" I told her.

"Well, you're all invited for the weekend!"

There were four of us—myself, songwriter Steve Schalchlin, and Manhattan real estate brokers Midge LaGuardia and Rolande Cicurel. Steve had met Lucy many times, but Midge and Rolande had not, and were very excited about spending time with one of their favorite stars. We pulled up to the gate of the Thunderbird Country Club and pushed the number Lucy told us.

"Well, it's about time!" rumbled her voice through the speaker. "Drive around to the right!" The gate opened, and we drove around to the right. Lucy was in the driveway in front of the modest house, holding Tinker in one hand and waving us in with the other.

Midge looked at her and said, "I don't believe what I'm seeing. Lucille Ball is waving at us." They all hit it off at once. Gary's sister, Helen Maurer, was waiting inside.

Lucy walked in front of us. "Come here! I want to show you the bathroom."

"I don't have to go," I said.

She rolled her eyes. "I don't want you to *go*. I want you to *look*."

She took us through a long corridor that featured a wonderful painting of Lucy surrounded by different aspects of her career. At the end of the corridor was Lucy and Gary's bedroom, and off to one side, the bathroom. I knew why she wanted us to see it. The room was divided into the actual bathroom part, with all the necessary fixtures, and a dressing room/office. That's right, an office in the bathroom. There was a desk, phone, shelves, and a walk-in closet. The wall was covered with pictures. Lucy loved to have tons of pictures all over her walls. Her grandchildren had the lion's share of space.

"Desi won this place in a gin game."

"Who was he playing?"

"I don't remember really. It was either George Goodyear or George Firestone or George somebody. They got into an all-night gin game at the clubhouse, and by the time they were both ready to drop, the guy owed Desi eighteen thousand dollars. Instead of paying him off in cash, he asked Desi if he wanted to have these two lots. They were worth nine thousand dollars apiece then. Desi loved real estate. He knew it was surefire, so he took them. We both designed the house they way we wanted. Let's walk around."

Lucy opened one of the long glass doors that led to the patio. The view was breathtaking. A small bridge separated their lot from the seventeenth fairway. A few golfers were looking for lost balls. Beyond the fairway, rising dramatically in the distance, were the San Gorgonio Mountains. There was a modest pool to the right of the patio. Lucy led the four of us past the pool, around to the back. When she turned around and saw us following in a single file, she did a funny little step and spun around. She looked back at us and did it again. I didn't get it at first, and then it dawned on me. She was playing Follow the Leader.

I repeated her funny step and spin, and the others did the same. When she saw us all doing what she was doing, she started walking like Chaplin, getting up and down on one knee and doing the Woody Woodpecker laugh. I kept thinking that if anyone saw us, he would think we had just escaped from the nuthouse.

Lucy pointed to a deep crevice in the ground. "That's where I had the scariest experience of my life. I was down here with

Norman and his wife [Dr. and Mrs. Norman Vincent Peale], and we had an earthquake. I don't mean an earthquake, I mean an EARTHQUAKE!! I was coming back in the house from a swim, and everything started shaking. It didn't knock me over, but it almost did. Then right there . . . it just opened up. The earth just pulled apart. It was like a studio would do special effects. I thought I was going to fall in, and the earth would swallow me up. And the sound. The sound was not to be believed. I thought that was it! Then it all stopped. God."

Steve and the girls joined Helen in the living room, and I went into the kitchen to help Lucy make lemonade. I was about to find out the secret of Lucy's lemonade, and we were about to have our first and only fight. When Lucy had it in her mind how something should be done, it was hard to change it. She took a can of frozen lemonade out of the freezer, opened it, and dumped the contents into a pitcher. She took a second can and repeated the process. "Put in two cans of water," she said as she handed me the empty lemonade can. "I'll get the Sweet 'n Low."

I looked at the instructions on the can, and it said to add four cans of water. I added one can of water, then two cans, and as I was about to add the third . . . "What are you doing?"

"I'm putting in two more cans of water!"

"No! You only need two!" she said sharply.

"It says four!"

"They're wrong."

"It's their lemonade!"

"They don't have to drink it!" She took the pitcher from me and added *six* packets of Sweet 'n Low.

"Are you trying to poison us?"

She stirred the potion and said, "Get the plastic glasses in the cupboard."

"I think we should have real glass," I said. "This will eat through plastic. No wonder you make the worst lemonade in the world." I felt as if I had been transported into the Ricardo kitchen as Lucy turned into "Lucy."

"What? I know how to make lemonade better than anybody in the world."

"Oh yeah?" I shot back. "If you did, you'd start with real lemons." She was getting annoyed. I thought it was funny. She poured a little into a cup and said, "Taste it!"

"I'm not going to taste it. You taste it!"

"Why won't you taste it?" she said with her hands on her hips.

"Because I want to live!"

She was exasperated. "Really!" She stomped her foot.

I took the sample out of her hand, drank it, and fell to the kitchen floor holding my stomach and screaming. The others came to the door. "What's the matter? What's the matter?"

I said, "Lucy poisoned me," and expired on the floor. After a beat, I looked up and went right into her old Vita-meta-vegamin routine, "Hello, friends. Do you poop out at parties? Are you unpopular? Then try Lucy's lemonade. It's so tasty, too!"

Lucy shouted, "Well, it is!" She poured herself a glass and took a big swig. Her body went through a series of involuntary spasms as she tried to get it down.

"How does it taste, O great lemonade-maker?"

She finally got her mouth uncontorted and said, "It needs more Sweet 'n Low." We all howled.

We went back to the living room and sat down around the backgammon table. The six of us were going to play each other in what is called a chouette, in which five players would play against one or we would play in teams of three. We would play for two days, and I knew the scoring would be hell. Lucy looked at me. "Jim, you keep score!"

After about four hours of play, the score was totally fouled up. Einstein couldn't have straightened it out. Steve got out the camera and took a picture of Lucy looking over my shoulder trying to find the mistake. We did. After that, we needed a break.

Helen, Midge, and Rolande decided to go out for a smoke. The smokers were relegated to the patio. Steve and I stayed with Lucy. I asked her if Little Lucie and Desi, Jr., came to Palm Springs often. She shook her head no.

"I don't think they like the house a lot. It has some bad memories."

"Like what?"

"Like you're sitting exactly where they were sitting the night Desi and I told them we were splitting up. They didn't understand 'splitting up.' Lucie looked at us and said, 'You can split up, just don't get divorced.'"

In 1959, *I Love Lucy* and the Arnaz marriage were coming to an end. The last straw came on a weekend trip to Del Mar. Lucy and Desi had a small house on the ocean. It was near the racetrack, where Desi loved to spend most of his time. Their neighbors were Jimmy and Marge Durante, and a lady named Edith Mack Hirsch. They all spent a lot of time together.

Lucy said, "I was always giving Desi a second chance, third chance, fourth chance, hundredth chance. I even thought when we got back from Capri, we could try again. But Desi was hell-bent on destroying himself, and when he started endangering the kids' lives, too, I knew it was over. On that last weekend at Del Mar, Jimmy and Marge were over at the house with their daughter CeCe. CeCe was about the same age as Lucie and Little Desi—a sweet child, who was the apple of Jimmy's eye. Edie Hirsch's marriage was on the rocks, and so she would spend a lot of time with us, too. One afternoon, Desi came back from the track with Jimmy. Jimmy was fine, but Desi was smashed (as usual). He changed into his trunks and told Little Desi to come for a swim with him. Desi would have done anything to spend time with his dad, and the two of them plunged into the surf. At first they were close to the shore, but Desi started to swim out, and Little Desi watched him go. His dad goaded him on to join him. Little Desi was petrified, but didn't want to say no to his father. Durante came up to me and said they were in trouble. Desi was close to his dad, and they kept going out further and further. If anything happened, Desi was in no shape to save anyone. I went down to the shore and started screaming. Little Lucie started crying. Desi and his dad got back to the beach, but the poor kid was winded and coughing up water. I wanted to kill his father right there in front of everyone. We cut the weekend short and came back to the house, and a pipe broke and Desi went wild. I'd never seen anything like it before or after. I was scared for my life. That did it. I knew I couldn't take anymore.

"We tried to protect the kids as long as we could. We would say good night and go into our bedroom together, but I would sleep in the big bed, and Desi would sleep in a bed in the dressing room. We would try to keep up a front, which was more draining than anything else. Besides being married, we were in business together, and business was terrific."

Business *was* great. Lucy was still reeling from the fact that she now owned the studio at which she had learned her craft. The main dressing suite that had once belonged to the studio's biggest star, Ginger Rogers, was now hers. In the deal, they had also acquired the Selznick studios in Culver City where Lucy had done her drenched audition for *Gone With the Wind*.

"The day we bought RKO was the same day we filmed the Tallulah show. Tallulah caused me so much *tsuris* that I just wanted to crawl in bed for a few days and stay there. Desi went off to work the next day, and all the newspapers were filled with stories about the acquisition. Desi called from Culver City and told me I had to come over for some publicity pictures. That's the last thing I wanted to do. I had no makeup on. My hair was in curlers. I was a mess. Desi insisted. He told me that it had to be done. The reporters would be there in an hour, and if I didn't show up, they would think there was trouble. We had to keep up a front. I could get my makeup and hair done at the studio."

Lucy jumped in the car and headed down Washington Boulevard into Culver City, and immediately got lost. With all the publicity about RKO being taken over by Desilu, all the employees were already worried about their jobs. When Lucy pulled up at the studio gate in babushka and dark glasses, the elderly security guard didn't recognize her at first and wouldn't let her pass.

She took off the sunglasses, and the poor old man's eyes popped out of his head as he realized he was face-to-face with his new boss. The flustered man didn't know whether to call her Mrs. Arnaz or Miss Ball, and so, with a sweeping gesture, he passed her through the gate and yelled, "Go right in Miss Arballs!"

The Desilu empire was growing by leaps and bounds. Now, in 1959, Desilu was about to launch one of its most successful series ever. It was called *The Untouchables*, based on the book by former federal agent Eliot Ness. Ness, the son of a Swedish immigrant, gained fame by successfully enforcing prohibition in Chicago during the Roaring Twenties. Ness's book had saved him from obscurity. After his famous confrontation with Al Capone, Ness retired to western Pennsylvania, where he ran for mayor of a small town and lost. A few years after that, the famous prohibitionist was arrested for drunk driving.

Desi thought that there was a great series in Ness's story, and obtained the rights. His first choice for the part of Eliot Ness was Van Johnson. Johnson had been a chorus boy in *Too Many Girls* with Desi in 1939. He was brought to Hollywood by RKO to appear in the chorus of the film. Although Van had no lines or billing, the audience picked him out of the crowd and labeled him a star. The label stuck.

Lucy had very ambivalent feelings about Johnson. At one time, they were close friends. He even appeared as a guest on *I Love Lucy*, where they sang and danced a duet of "How About You?"

"I liked Van, but I thought he was a very selfish man. He had turned from a sweet kid into an egomaniac. Keenan and Evie Wynn and I were friends. I worked with Keenan on *Without Love* with Tracy and Hepburn, and he was a swell guy. I did a small bit with his dad [Ed Wynn] when I first got to Hollywood, and met Keenan then but didn't get to know him until the late forties. One night Van was over, and he said he was in love with Evie. He couldn't live without her. I said, 'Evie who?' He said, 'Evie Wynn!' I couldn't believe he was serious. I always thought that Keenan and Evie had a good marriage, but then I found out that Van had gotten her pregnant. She divorced Keenan and married Van, and once the baby was born, Van didn't pay much attention to either one of them. I spoke to him after that, but I didn't think much of him."

When Van was offered the part of Eliot Ness, Evie was his manager. They made a deal for ten thousand dollars for Van to appear in the pilot. When Evie found out the pilot would be shown in two parts, she called Desi and insisted that Van be paid ten thousand dollars for each part. Desi hit the ceiling. He canceled Van on the spot and hired Robert Stack.

Lucy also hit the ceiling when Desi told her that a suggestion had been made to add realism to the show. The suggestion was that Walter Winchell narrate each episode. "I never felt so betrayed. Here was the man who had called me a communist, and now we were supposed to turn around and give him a job. Jesus!"

Despite Lucy's objections, Winchell got the job, and once again Desi was right about his adding the right touch to the show. Desi offered the show to CBS, but when William Paley watched it, he couldn't see its potential. He refused the show, and ABC grabbed on to one of the biggest hits in the history of television.

Lucy didn't have the strength to keep up the front about the state of her marriage anymore. Aside from the heartache she knew the kids would go through, she also knew she would be disappointing millions of fans who saw Desi and her as the most married couple in America. She couldn't go on with *I Love Lucy* any longer, and it seemed like the perfect time—Lucy would end the show and her marriage at the same time.

The last show featured Ernie Kovacs and his second wife, Edie Adams. The rehearsals started with Lucy and Desi screaming at each other, and ended by them talking to each other only through third parties. The final scene called for Desi and Lucy to kiss. The kiss lasted longer than rehearsed. Lucy was not going to melt again. She broke the kiss and said to Desi, "Aren't you going to yell, 'cut'?"

Desi called cut on the show and on the marriage. He came back to the house on Roxbury Drive that night only to pick up his clothes. He told Lucy he would not fight her. They took the children to Palm Springs the following weekend to break the news to them. Lucy said, "They were very hip kids for their ages. Desi was six and Lucie was eight, but they were in schools where other parents had gotten divorced. They had friends whose parents tried to kill each other over a divorce. They were afraid. We promised them that we would be friends, but [said] that we couldn't be married anymore. They cried for a week. I cried for a month."

Lucy filed for divorce on March 3, 1960. It was uncontested by Desi and finalized quickly.

I took Lucy's hand as she looked around the Palm Springs living room. She said, "The divorce was painful, but not as painful as the marriage."

Helen, Midge, and Rolande came back in from having their cigarettes. Lucy sighed, got up, crossed back to the backgammon table, and we continued to play.

CHAPTER
Fifteen

THE SECOND DAY of our Palm Springs First Annual Backgammon Tournament was in financial chaos. I was still keeping track of the score, and between Steve at -78, Rolande at $+42$, Midge at -37, Jim at $+16$, Helen at $+212$, Lucy at -1, and Tinker even, at a quarter a point, we were totally screwed up. If the score was right, we each owed

Helen $112,000. Every time I'd announce the new score, everyone would howl!

Lucy took charge. But it wasn't our friend Lucy, it was "Lucy" in character, trying to get Ethel Mertz to get the score right. At this performance, *I* was Ethel Mertz.

"What's the matter with you? Can't you add?" she said, putting her hands on her hips and tapping her foot.

"Yes," I said, slowly and deliberately, "I can add all right. I just can't keep score."

"Well, it's not that difficult!"

"Oh, it's not? Well, then," I said, handing her the scorecard, "*you* keep score, Miss Einstein of '34."

She grabbed the score out of my hand. "All right. I will." She turned it one way, then another. "I know where you went wrong."

"So do I. When I said I'd come over this afternoon."

"Look. Right here." She was so sure of herself. "You went wrong with Helen."

"Who didn't?"

She stomped her foot. "Now, look, I'm serious. You went wrong three games ago. You gave Helen too much and . . ."

Helen (playing the role of Fred Mertz) chimed in, "No, he didn't. I'll keep score."

Lucy stomped again. "Sit down, Helen." Helen sat.

Lucy took the pad in her hand and started mumbling, "Seven times twenty-six . . . no that's not it. Er, you were partners with Midge, and Helen was in the box . . . no, that's not it. If you take two and divide it into . . ."

I took the pad back. "See, Miss Smarty-pants? It's not so easy, is it? I don't think you can add, either."

"I can't!"

"How could you run a studio and not be able to add?"

She looked at me as if I were crazy. "I hired somebody who could." The scene couldn't go any higher than that. She got the biggest laugh of the day, so we broke for lunch.

We were picking at leftover turkey, and I asked her if Gary was going to be back from playing golf so he could eat with us.

"No, he'll be a while. It takes time to drive back."

I asked Lucy why he didn't play golf on his own course.

Lucy scowled. "Because he's Jewish."

"You mean he can live here, but he can't play golf here?"

Lucy shook her head. "Or eat at the club-house."

"I don't believe it. I didn't think that still happened in this day and age."

"Believe it!"

I was agitated. "I think that's terrible. I think if he owns a house here, he should be allowed to do whatever he wants. He should sue them. Did he ever think of suing them?"

"Gary would never do that," she said, standing straight up. "He's a gentleman. A real gentleman."

It's true. Gary Morton is a gentleman. He is a soft-spoken, funny, straightforward man, who loved only one thing before he loved Lucy—show business. He and I had a favorite quote of Jackie Gleason, who once said on *The David Susskind Show*, "I didn't care if I had to shine actors' shoes, as long as I was in show business."

Gary was born Morton Goldapper in the Bronx in 1921. Morty went into the business as a stand-up comic. He told me, "I couldn't write the stuff myself, but I know what's funny. I'm a good editor of material, and I can deliver it well, but I can't write it. That's why I always appreciate good writers."

The fact that Desi stayed in Lucy's life after their divorce and that the public would forever have them linked as husband and wife in the chapel of reruns didn't seem to bother Gary at all. He knew the cherished place he held for Lucy both in public and in her heart, and he also knew the place that Desi held. From time to time, Lucy would get on a "Desi kick." "Desi did this and Desi did that . . ." Gary would roll his eyes and say, "She's referring to my ex-husband-in-law."

After Lucy filed for the divorce, it seemed to her she had made a mistake by keeping the problems from the children for so long. Everyone had been pretending that everything was all right, and then all of a sudden everything wasn't all right.

Just before they got divorced, they both agreed to go to a psychiatrist to see if there was any marriage left, and if they could possibly save it. It was only for the sake of the kids. After a few visits, it was obvious to both of them that it wasn't working. "Desi and I would scream and yell in front of the doctor because we weren't screaming and yelling in front of the children. I felt sorry for the poor guy. He'd ask a question, and the two of us would jump down his throat, and the war was on. Desi quit after a few weeks, and I kept on seeing him by myself.

I quit after a few weeks, because all he wanted to talk about was my childhood, but that was going nowhere, because I had a happy childhood."

The kids were devastated by the news. "They cried and cried, and, Jesus, I'll never forget the sound of those two kids weeping. That really stays with you. I never thought they would go to pieces like that. I wanted them to know that Desi was still going to be their father and they would see him whenever they wanted, and the only thing that would be different was that he wouldn't live with them anymore. I thought they knew what was going on, but they were little kids and we kept it from them, and so it was like a bomb dropped.

"I didn't want to come out and say, 'We got a divorce because he's a drunk and he lays every broad in Hollywood and comes home drunk every night and screams at me.' It was important for me that they know that *I* didn't cause the divorce. That it wasn't me who failed. I wanted to tell them, 'It's all your father's fault. Blame him!' I couldn't do it. I knew that if I told them to blame him, they'd only blame me anyway. I had to let them find out for themselves what their father was like. They had to experience it

218

for themselves. And unfortunately . . . they did."

If Lucy had underestimated the reaction of the children, she superunderestimated the reaction of the public. "Even when I was called a communist, a few nuts called me terrible things, but in general everybody was so supportive. They sent me great letters. But when Desi and I got divorced, it was unbelievable. They called me everything in the book. Others just begged for us not to do it. Everybody asked us to think it over. I couldn't believe that everybody in the United States had an opinion about our divorce."

Lucy needed a complete change. She wanted to get out of Hollywood, and told a few friends she was looking for a Broadway show. The dream of a fairy-tale marriage had failed, but she still had the dream of starring in a Broadway musical. A call came from N. Richard Nash. Lucy knew *The Rainmaker*, and thought he had something like the character of Lizzie (which Katharine Hepburn illuminated on the screen), and believed it would be an auspicious debut. She had no idea the dream of a smash Broadway musical would fail, but that she'd get a fairytale marriage out of it.

Lucy has always resisted change. Up until the day she died, she resisted having Touch-Tone telephones. She had the only phones in Hollywood with rotary dials. But in 1960, she was seeking a complete change. She found an apartment at the Imperial House at Sixty-ninth Street and Lexington Avenue. She picked out the colors and redid the whole place herself while waiting for rehearsals for *Wildcat* to start. She brought the kids with her and put them into parochial schools. Lucy was not a Catholic. She did not hold much for organized religion except for the positive-thinking philosophy of her friend Norman Vincent Peale. "Dr. Peale was great during that time. I kept looking at the divorce as a failure. He asked me one day if I thought my divorce was a crisis in my life. I thought it was a strange question, but I thought about it and, yes, it was certainly a personal crisis. He told me that the Chinese symbol for the word crisis was the combination of two other words—danger and opportunity. I thought about the significance of that. The divorce was dangerous for all of us . . . for me, Desi, and the kids. But it also presented opportunities. And I took them. I never missed an opportunity in my life.

"I put the kids into Catholic school because when we had gotten married again in the Church [in 1949], I promised that I would do it. I promised I would raise them Catholic. I didn't like to break contracts, and besides, I think it gave them some kind of an anchor." I once asked Lucy if she believed in an afterlife, and she looked at me, deeply into my eyes, before she answered silently. She shook her head back and forth, no, slowly and deliberately and somewhat sadly, as if she wished her answer were different.

Lucy was finding rehearsals for *Wildcat* harder than she anticipated. She had gone from a schedule of starting rehearsals for her TV show on a Monday morning and filming it on Thursday night, with three days off to do with what she wanted, to rehearsing eight hours a day for six days a week. The final week of rehearsal was twelve hours a day with no days off. "I was exhausted before the curtain ever went up."

Lucy did the best she could during rehearsals, relying on the scuttlebutt of the chorus boys to tell her what was working in the show and what wasn't. She didn't trust the director, Michael Kidd. "He didn't direct me into the show, he directed the show around me." She looked to her fellow actors and chorus kids for support, and found it. One of the girls in the chorus remembered her: "Lucy was terrific. She was very forthcoming, loving, warm, and insisted on meeting each individual as an individual." The chorus girl was Valerie Harper. (Another future star, Hal Linden, played saxophone in the pit orchestra.)

When the show opened in Philadelphia, the response was lukewarm; the response for Lucy was joyous. She was afraid that people would hate her because of the divorce and wouldn't want to see her in anything. They wanted to see her, but they wanted to see the Lucy they knew, not the tough, conniving Wildcat Jackson whom she was playing. "Philadelphia told us a lot. The slightest bit of 'Lucy' that I would throw in would get the reaction I was looking for. Nothing that man wrote got any laughs, and I was getting desperate and Kidd didn't tell me not to, so I did."

Wildcat opened at the Alvin Theatre in New York on December 16, 1960. The reviews for the show were tepid, but the critics loved Lucy. Desi was at the opening. It gave her strength to have him there. After five years of hell, they were getting along better than they ever had. The show was an instant hit, but the eight shows a week were taking a toll. All the ailments she once suffered —the osteomyelitis, the rheumatism, the dehydration, and the exhaustion—were coming back all at once. When she came down with the flu, the audiences would not accept the understudy, so the whole cast took a vacation while Lucy recovered.

She took the kids to Florida, and didn't move for a week. She needed a second week of rest to completely get back on her feet, but the threat of an airline strike made her go back to the show before she really wanted to. Instead of taking an extra night off before returning to work, she drummed up business by doing the opening number, "Hey, Look Me Over!," on *The Ed Sullivan Show* with Paula Stewart. Her first entrance was from under an ailing Stutz Bearcat, and she bumped her head badly as she emerged. She glossed over it by going, "Boing!," but it gave her a nasty bump. When the number was over, the crowd roared, and Ed brought her over to take a bow. He said, "You know, ladies and gentlemen, down through the years because of what she's given the country—all of the world, as a matter of fact—Lucille Ball, I would say that you are the most beloved star in show business." The audience cheered their approval.

While she was back in the show, she was missing married life. "I shouldn't have had time to think about romance, but I missed Desi. I even missed the fighting. It was something. I had the kids and I had my work, but I didn't have a rock. I didn't have that one person I could lean on. A very strange thing happened one night after a performance of *Wildcat*. I had been thinking about calling Desi and asking him to come to New York, but I didn't do it. One night the doorman came to my dressing room and said, 'Lucy, there is a couple here who would like to see you.'

" 'Do I know them?'

" 'No. They say they don't know you, but they said they have something that belongs to you and want you to have it.'

"I told him to let them in. My dressing room had a little sitting-room part to it, so I got changed, and the old man brought the couple in and sat them down in the dressing room. When I came out, I knew I had never met them before, but I said hello and asked them if they liked the show and all that. They were very polite and sweet. The lady said they had something they thought belonged to me. The man cut in and told me that he and his wife had just gone to Hawaii for their anniversary. They had never been, and how beautiful it was and all that stuff and . . . well, he told me that he and his wife went swimming one evening at the beach and he thought he caught his leg on seaweed. When they got out of the water, he reached down his leg and found this. The lady opened her purse and pulled out a gold chain with a Saint Christopher medal and a wedding ring. I looked in the ring, and it read, 'To Desi with Love from Lucy.' It was the ring Desi had lost almost two years before. I thanked them, kissed them both, and then closed the door and wept. Just sat there and wept. It's funny, but it was then that I knew it was really over. Having that ring in my hands didn't bring the good times back to me, it brought the terrible times back, and I knew it was right. I knew Desi and I could be friends, but that we shouldn't be married."

Lucy got up from the backgammon table and came back a few minutes later with the ring and the medal.

"Didn't you ever tell Desi you found it?"

"No. I didn't. I've kept it. I want Desi [Jr.] to have it."

Lucy's timing had always been impeccable, but this time it proved to be true of her love life as well. Paula Stewart, who played Janie, Wildy's kid sister in *Wildcat*, had become a friend. Lucy gravitated to the same kind of people as herself for friendship. Paula was down-to-earth, energetic, full of life, and loved to laugh. She was married to one of the top comedians in the business, Jack Carter.

Lucy enjoyed Jack because he was funny offstage. He thought funny. He had funny friends. One of them was Gary Morton, who then was the opening act for Nat King Cole. When he wasn't working with Nat, Gary was doing seven shows a day at the Radio City Music Hall and traveling to the Catskills for shows on the weekend. He was working all the time, making a good living but in Borscht Belt hotels and New York clubs, not on television, where he could get exposure. Consequently, the public didn't know who he was.

Jack brought Gary around to meet Lucy, and the four of them went out for pizza. Gary had all the qualities that Lucy liked. And he was tall. She loved tall men. He could also make her laugh. She told me, "Gary makes me laugh most in bed. Noooooo! I don't mean that. I meant he thinks of funny things in bed. I woke up last night, and he was sound asleep, so I just leaned over on him and started chanting in his ear . . . Ohhhhh-mmmmmmmmmmmmmmmmmmmmmmmmm-mmmmmm! [She went on for thirty seconds.] Gary finally looked around at her and said, 'Man River.'" Lucy thought that was hilarious.

Gary was instantly attracted to her. "Lucy had that quality like Carole Lombard. She was gorgeous. Glamorous. Absolutely beautiful. But she didn't care how she looked if it got a laugh."

After the pizza night, they sent funny telegrams to each other. They went out without Paula and Jack. They had an affair. They got married.

Gary had seen Lucy on television only a few times during her nine-year stint. "I was always out or asleep on Monday night." They went to Lucy's friend Dr. Peale, and he approved. They flew out for Gary to meet Desi. He also approved. The kids saw the marriage coming before anyone else. They also knew that this was a very different man from their father. He was not given to rages of temper; rather, he would sit and consider a situation and give a thoughtful answer. He was not a big drinker subject to pendulous mood swings. He was kind and gentle with their mother.

Even though everyone had said okay, Lucy wasn't sure. "When you've disappointed so many people and got burned so badly, you don't go running off in a week!" It was a year.

Lucy went to the top and introduced Gary to DeDe, who gave her ultimate blessing, and they drove to Marble Collegiate Church on Twenty-eighth and Fifth to be married by Dr. Peale. Gary knew Lucy was a famous actress, but not *how* famous. When the limousine carrying Gary, Lucy, Little Lucie, and Desi, Jr., turned the corner of Twenty-seventh Street to come around in front of the church, the street looked like Times Square on New Year's Eve. The car could barely get through the crowd. Gary turned to Lucy, astonished yet oblivious, and mused, "I wonder who they're waiting for?"

CHAPTER
Sixteen

LUCY WAS IN New York for a week and called me. "I wish you were here," she said.

I asked her where she was calling from

and she said from her New York apartment on the twenty-sixth floor overlooking the East River. She told me she had seen *Phantom of the Opera* and met Michael Crawford. She was very excited about that. She also told me that she had seen my old friend Charles Pierce's act the night before, and he'd taken some snapshots, which he would send me.

She was anxious to come home. New York wasn't the same town she'd once loved. She missed California—the same way she did when *Wildcat* closed in August of 1961. New York had been a healing experience, and she had found her rock amid the concrete. Gary's family was from New York, and they had to break the news to Gary's mother that they would live in California, not New York.

Helen Goldapper Maurer says that when she found out she was going to be Lucille Ball's sister-in-law, she couldn't believe it. She'd always felt a special affinity to Lucy, because she gave birth to her daughter Randi the same night that Lucy had Little Ricky on TV and Little Desi in real life. "When Lucy was having labor pains on the screen, I was having them on the sofa. But I was laughing so hard I didn't want to go to the hospital until the show was over."

Lucy wanted Gary's family to come for

dinner before they went back to California. Lucy knew that Gary's mother, Rose, loved chopped chicken livers, and it was one of Lucy's specialties. She slaved in the kitchen all day, preparing the big dinner for her new mother-in-law. Rose rang the downstairs bell. Lucy took her plate of chopped liver out of the refrigerator and brought it to the counter. "I was doing fine. Right on time, but I hadn't put the chopped egg on top yet. So I put the egg on it, and it was beautiful. I tasted it with the egg, and it needed just a dash more salt. I reached for the salt thing, sprinkled it over the egg, and bam! The top came off and the salt poured out. It looked like a giant snowbank on top of the chicken livers. Now, they're getting off the elevator, and I don't know what to do. You know what I did?"

"What did you do?"

"I rinsed it! I put it under the faucet and rinsed it, and all the chicken livers disintegrated and went right down the drain. It was terrible. I think I ruined everything that night. In fact, we went out to eat."

Lucy became very fond of Rose, and invited her to visit them in California. Rose took them up on their offer and flew out to the Coast. They went to Palm Springs for a weekend party at the home of Frank Sinatra. Rose sat in Frank Sinatra's living room with her purse squarely on her lap. She chatted with Sammy Davis, Jr., Peter Lawford, and Old Blue Eyes himself. Gary sat next to his mother to point out the celebrities. "I whispered in her ear. I said, 'Ma, do you know who that lady is sitting next to you?' She looked at the woman but didn't recognize her. I said, 'Ma, that's Pat Kennedy Lawford. Her brother is the president of the United States.' My mother says, 'Is that so?,' and turns around to her and says, 'Excuse me, Mrs. Pat Kennedy Lawford.' Pat was a little startled but very gracious, and I introduced them. My mother says, 'You know, Mrs. Pat Kennedy Lawford, it just so happens that I know your brother the president very well.' Pat looked at her a moment and said, 'You know my brother?'

" 'That's right.'

" 'How do you know my brother?'

"My mother leaned over to Pat and very confidentially whispered, 'He gave a speech in my neighborhood!' "

The return to California took adjustment. Gary was now the man of the house, and the children would answer to him. He learned the part of parent very well. Lucie and Desi still loved their dad, but respected Gary and treated him the same as Lucy did, as the head of the house.

It seems as though every time Lucy swore she would never do something, she went out and did it. She swore she would never do another series. She swore that four times. With her marriage stable and the kids adjusting to the new guy, she had to go back to work.

Although they were divorced, Lucy and Desi were still business partners. Desilu was doing all right—just. It needed a hit, and Desi asked Lucy to come back to TV. CBS jumped at the chance to have her back, and ordered a series with no pilot and no scripts for an entire season. Lucy wanted her "group" back. She tried not to change any of the formula that made the first show work, but she needed to make adjustments. Desi went back to the book he had optioned some years before called *Life Without George*, about a widow raising her children. It was perfect. Lucy wanted Vivian to play her sidekick, but Vivian was reluctant.

For years, Vivian had been the ugly duckling to Lucy's glamour girl. It was in her *I Love Lucy* contract that she would have to stay twenty pounds overweight and wear dumpy dresses. Lucy didn't want Vivian to be attractive. Hal King used to make Vivian up during the *I Love Lucy* years until Lucy put a stop to it because Hal was making Vivian too glamorous.

Vivian also found happiness in a second marriage and her husband, John Dodds, was a publisher whose business was firmly rooted in New York. If Lucy wanted Vivian to come back to California, she would have to pay plenty and elevate Vivian to being her fashion equal. Lucy said that she never knew what Vivian's salary was, and she didn't want to know. She thought it would have made her angry. "But whatever it was, she deserved it."

Vivian also insisted on wardrobe approval and that her character's name would be Vivian, not Ethel Mae. Lucy agreed to whatever Viv wanted in order to have her back. Lucy believed in nepotism. She wanted the people she knew and trusted around her, people who knew her strengths and weaknesses and who didn't take her tantrums and flare-ups seriously. Jack Donahue (her director) was back, along with Desi as producer, Vivian as costar, Hal King doing her makeup, her writers, Madelyn and Bob, and her "sister" (cousin), Cleo. Everybody was there but Gary.

She explained that she didn't exclude Gary because he was not capable; quite the contrary. She knew he was able to do almost any job, but believed the public would not share her impression. "I didn't want to take a man who was his own man who had a wonderful ego and deflate it in any way. I didn't want him to become Mr. Ball. I took the precaution of saying that Gary will have no part of the business end until I'm sure he can handle it. I knew he had the stuff, but they didn't know."

Gary stood on the sidelines watching and learning how to be an executive producer. He watched for five years. In the meantime, he found a place for himself on the set doing what he did best. He warmed up the audience before the show began. From time to time, he made a cameo appearance. Lucie once said, "Whenever we needed an emcee for the PTA show, Gary had the job."

Lucy had an unfulfilled dream that she could realize with the acquisition of RKO. She always remembered the wonderful training that Lela Rogers had given the young contract players at the studio, and she wanted to do the same. The Little Theatre was still standing on what was now the De-silu lot, and Lucy wanted to bring it back to life.

She put an ad in the Hollywood trade papers that Desilu was starting an apprentice program for young actors and actresses. She had room for twenty-two students, who would take classes, study scenes, appear in small parts in the Desilu shows and be paid for them. Lucy modeled the program on the techniques she learned from the RKO classes and the John Murray Anderson School. She insisted that the kids be paid. Several hundred young performers responded to the ad. Lucy auditioned each one personally, and chose all twenty-two herself.

Robert Osborne, a noted columnist for *The Hollywood Reporter*, was part of that first group of students. A few days after Lucy's death, he wrote a moving tribute to her, remembering what it was like to have Lucy as a teacher. "We were mostly newcomers to Hollywood. There was Carole Cook, Marilyn Lovell, Gary Menteer, Georgine Darcy, Howard Storm, Ken Berry, Jerry Antes. Lucy often had us to her house en masse, or singularly, and she'd cluck over us like a mother hen. 'Are you getting enough sleep? Are you eating enough? Are you happy?'

Through the years, she often called, checking up on us or just to say something nice. Lucy was a long-term friend/surrogate mama to many of us."

Lucy loved to teach. She was contradictory in one of her statements. She always said you can't teach somebody to be funny, and at the same time she never thought of herself as funny. "You can teach somebody how to do a take, how to walk funny, how to mug, and stuff like that, but you can't teach people how to react to something in a funny way. Reacting is most of it."

Lucy produced full shows in the Little Theatre, and invited all of the Hollywood press to come and review the proceedings. She paced back and forth in the lobby smoking cigarette after cigarette, worrying like a New York producer on opening night.

Although she was encouraging young talent at the studio, she was discouraging her own young talent at home. The kids wanted to be in the business, and Lucy treated them the way Ricky treated "Lucy." Lucy didn't want them in the spotlight. She insisted they stay home and be normal children.

Lucy approved of putting on shows at home. She had done the same thing as a child, performing *Charley's Aunt* in the garage for a penny a customer. Sometimes the only customer she had was her dog, but the show went on regardless. Little Lucie and Desi, Jr., put on revues in the garage with the neighborhood children, and Lucy saw that the kids were talented. Still, she wanted to protect them from the trauma that went along with child stardom. She would tell them when they were ready.

She had reels of film from when the kids were babies. The projection rooms in both the Los Angeles and Palm Springs houses were not so much for the studio films they would occasionally screen, as for the *85,000 feet* of home movies. There were the traditional birthday and pony-ride films, and others that included full-costume dramas. One 8 mm was called *The Fat Little Cowboy*. The plot was simple. Lucie (age four) and Desi (age two and a half) are sitting on a bench wearing overalls and cowboy hats. Lucie waves, takes Desi by the hand, and leads him to a chaise lounge. They sit. I told Lucy I thought the plot was almost Kafkaesque in its simplicity.

Lucy said, "I agree," and looked at me as if I had just landed from Pluto.

She said that she encouraged her children to learn the business, but didn't want to put them in it before they were ready. "I have very creative children. They were always trying something. They were always inquisitive. They always had something going."

We took a break from the game and went into the kitchen for lemonade. As soon as she reached into the refrigerator for the pitcher, we both thought of our Palm Springs lemonade war and started laughing. She held out the pitcher. "You can drink this. Frank made it."

"I wouldn't drink it if the pope made it with holy water!" I yelled. She was already starting to double up laughing. "I wouldn't care who made the stuff, because they make it the way you tell them to . . . with a half a can of water and twenty-two Sweet 'n Lows." That did it. She laughed so hard, her face turned the same color as her hair.

She finally managed to get a few words out. "Well, if that's the way you feel, you'll never be offered lemonade in this house again."

I fell to the floor on my knees and started kissing her hand, "Thank you, missus. Thank you. That's the kindest thing you've ever said to me."

Frank, Roza, and Chris were now in the doorway, wondering why we were both howling. Who would have thought lemonade could be so funny?

As we sat down to play again, Lucy was reminded of the hot summer when her kids decided to go into the lemonade business and she found out just how creative her children were.

When *The Lucy Show* went into production, it was August. A very hot August. Little Lucie and Desi, Jr., decided to clean up on the number of thirsty tourists who would buy maps to the movie stars' homes and wander the streets of Beverly Hills.

Lucy said she and Gary would leave for the studio early in the morning, and come home to find the kids had made a small fortune selling lemonade at a dime a glass. They each had fistfuls of ten- and twenty-dollar bills. After a week, she found out the kids had not made their fortunes in lemonade but were instead giving tours of the house for a dollar a peep.

The hoax was exposed by Willie Mae, Lucy's housekeeper, who found a group of strangers meandering around Lucy's bathroom. She asked the people what they were doing there. One of the ladies looked her up and down, snapped off a picture, and told her, "We're on the tour!"

Desi had taken the house in Del Mar so he could be near the ocean and the racetrack. Lucy loved the Palm Springs house and kept that. Gary and Lucy took the kids there for the Christmas break. They made the drive in two hours. Lucy was not used to the car trip. She had fringe benefits by being the producer of *Whirlybirds,* an adventure series about helicopter pilots. One of the choppers crashed, and a pilot was killed. Lucy never used a helicopter after that.

The four of them went to the Racquet Club for Christmas Eve lunch, and on the way out ran into former President Eisenhower and his wife, Mamie. Eisenhower shook hands with Desi, Jr., and said, "Are you the young man who upstaged my first inauguration?"

Desi was dumbstruck as the five-star general-president pumped his hand. Lucy laughed as she remembered it. "I think he scared the poor little thing to death."

Lucy enjoyed holidays because they gave her a chance to be a kid again. The family would always do something special for Easter and in December outline the house in white Christmas lights, but Lucy's favorite was Halloween. "We used to do up Halloween like nobody's business. We'd put eerie green lights outside the house and set up speakers that had blowing wind and screams. We'd all dress up and have all different kinds of candy and treats. We would jump out from behind the bushes. We had a great bunch of kids every year . . . the Levant girls from down the street and Candy Bergen from around the corner and Jeanne Crain's kids from across the street. [Lucy was struck with a thought as she spoke.] God, Jeanne Crain had so many kids. And they were always over here, and for some reason . . . they were always sick." She sighed. "I miss them." Then she looked at me and added, "The holidays, not Jeanne Crain's kids."

The more Lucy's life stabilized, the more Desi's was unraveling. When he wasn't overseeing every phase of every part of production on all the Desilu shows, he was gambling or getting laid. Through all of it, he was drinking more heavily than ever. Desi had built an empire but destroyed himself in the process. He was hospitalized with an assortment of acute illnesses ranging from liver disease to bleeding ulcers and had to undergo a colostomy.

Desi made a decision to get out of the business altogether. He finally realized his life was in danger, and he had to slow down or die. As part of the divorce settlement, the Arnazes agreed that if one wanted to sell his or her shares of Desilu, the seller would offer them to the other partner first. Desi would have done that anyway. He offered Lucy a deal to buy him out. He practically gave her the shares for a couple of million dollars.

Lucy never thought of herself as smart, because she didn't have a high school diploma, but she had a doctorate in street smarts from the School of Life. She seized the chance to take over the studio. She had seen many actors who once had power and clout in the industry walking around with their hands out because they'd missed opportunities to take control of their own lives and their own futures. Lucy would not let that happened to her or her kids. She would become president of the studio, and she would hire herself and her relatives to work for her.

She saw that Gary was learning to be a producer, and along with Art Monella, her accountant, would keep an eye on the business end of production. Lucy would throw herself into the creative end by finding projects that she liked for friends she wanted to work with, and above all develop new talent and provide showcases for it.

Desi went to Del Mar, where he ran into Edie Hirsch. They had been neighbors for years, and had a mutual love of the track. Since Edie had divorced her husband, Clement, Desi asked her out for dinner and the races. They found good companions in each other. Desi could do for Edie what Gary could do for Lucy . . . make her laugh. Desi was off the booze and relaxing, and found things to laugh at once again.

Since the kids already knew Edie for years and liked her, Desi returned Lucy's compliment and asked her what she thought about his remarriage. Lucy liked Edie. They were girlfriends and always got along. Lucy was pleased. Bringing Edie into the family would not change the scheme of things all that much. She gave her blessing.

Desi and Edie flew to Las Vegas and were married on March 2, 1963, at the Sands Hotel. Lucy sent them a flowered horseshoe with a sash that read, CONGRATULATIONS ON BOTH OF YOU PICKING A WINNER.

CHAPTER
Seventeen

I LEFT THE house one afternoon about five-thirty. I had to pick up a friend who was waiting for me. I turned the ignition, and nothing. My car was dead. I went back into the house and said, "My battery is dead. I have to call a garage."

Lucy peeked through the shutters in the den to have a look. "Maybe Chris can give you a jump."

Chris and his wife, Roza, a very attractive couple in their midthirties, had been on Lucy's staff for a year. They are a charming couple, eager to please, easy to make laugh. Sometimes when Lucy and I were playing on a Saturday afternoon, we would hear screams coming from the laundry room. Lucy and I would run through the kitchen into the corridor and find Roza standing at the ironing board laughing out loud at a *Lucy* rerun she was watching on a small black-and-white television. "Sorry, madam," she would say to Lucy, "but you are very funny." Lucy would walk back to the living room shaking her head and wearing the broadest smile.

Lucy thought Chris bowed too much. He was very Continental and wished everyone *"Bon appétit!"* as he served dinner. She wasn't sure of him. She might have been the queen of Hollywood, but she was uncomfortable with the help clicking their heels and wishing her. *"Bon appétit!"* every time she lifted a fork.

She changed her attitude about Chris the Saturday before Thanksgiving. My friend Mort Schwartz, Lucy, and I were playing in the den when we heard a tremendous crash. The house had been so quiet moments before that the sound made us all get up at once and run to see what happened.

At first, we thought it was a tourist trying to break in, but when we got to the hallway, we saw Chris lying at the foot of the stairs, moaning. He had been cleaning the brass rail on the stairs leading to the second floor. He was just outside Lucy and Gary's bedroom when he slipped and fell the whole length of the stairs.

Lucy insisted Chris go to the hospital to have his arm looked at. He didn't understand the directions I was trying to give, so Lucy suggested I drive to the hospital and let Chris and Roza follow me in their car. I dropped them off in front of the Cedars-Sinai emergency room and went back to Lucy's to await word.

Lucy was worried about Chris. She called the hospital to check on his condition but couldn't get any information. After three hours, they returned.

Lucy got upset when she saw the cast on his arm, but Chris assured her that the injury wasn't as serious as it looked. It was a minor fracture. Still, he was obviously in a lot of pain.

Lucy told him to get some rest. She and Gary sat down for dinner a few minutes later, and Chris served the entire meal, cast and all. No matter how much Lucy pleaded with him, he would not rest his arm until all of his duties were performed.

Chris came out to jump-start my car. I was now ten minutes late. He tried and tried, but the car wouldn't start.

We went back into the house, and I told Lucy I was going to call a garage. She thought that was a bad idea. "You'll be late. You don't have time." She handed me a key ring. "Take *my* car. Just bring it back to-morrow, and we'll get yours going then."

My mind started to race—was it the Rolls?

Or the Bentley? Which one of the Mercedes? I asked her, "What car do you want me to take?"

"Frank is bringing it around."

I heard the engine get louder as it made the turn out of the garage and into the driveway. A shiny white '86 Chrysler.

I felt like the contestant on *Let's Make a Deal* who picked the wrong door. "This is *your* car?"

"Yeah. We usually keep it in Palm Springs. Frank will drive it there so we can have it for the weekend, but Gary won't let me drive it."

"Why?"

"I don't know. I can't do anything anymore. Just drive carefully. And don't let it get the last word."

"The last word? What do you mean?"

Lucy smiled and squinted a knowing look. "You'll see."

I opened the car door, and the car spoke. "Your left door is open. Your taillight is out. Please step in. Please fasten your seat belt. Please put your key in the ignition." I looked to see what model it was. It should have been "the Chrysler Mother-in-law . . . the car that never shuts up."

Lucy loved to drive. She always had a

chauffeur on staff. When they began *The Lucy Show*, Lucy's driver was Eddie. On the days when Lucy didn't need the five-mile drive through Beverly Hills and down Melrose Avenue to memorize her lines, she'd drive the car herself and have Eddie sit next to her.

Lucy got to drive her talking convertible once more before she died, and she wished she hadn't. While Lucy and Gary were spending a week in Palm Springs, Lucy made an appointment at the beauty parlor to have her hair done. She pleaded with Gary to let her drive herself. It wasn't L.A., so the traffic would be light, it wasn't far, it was a beautiful day—how much trouble could she get into? Plenty.

Gary said okay, so Lucy tied on her babushka, put on her sunglasses, and got into the talking car. She was in such a happy mood, she talked back to it.

"Your left door is ajar," said the car.

"Thanks," she answered. "Know any good jokes?"

Lucy pulled out of the country club driveway and onto the highway, elated to be behind the wheel again. She noticed that the traffic was unusually heavy for midweek and became irritated when the cars slowed to a crawl. As she approached the intersection of Bob Hope Drive and Route 111, the car conked out. Every system went dead, except for the one that operated the mechanical voice. With a herd of cars honking their horns at her, Lucy turned the key in the ignition over and over to no avail. She sat behind the wheel listening to the voice drone on, "Please fasten your seat belt. Your gas level is adequate. Cruise control is set at sixty-five miles an hour. Your door is still ajar!"

"Shut up," Lucy said, banging her fist against the dashboard. Above the din of the honking horns, Lucy could hear the siren of an approaching police car. A young lady patrol officer came around to the driver's side of the car and leaned in. Lucy, near tears, told the officer that the car had died on her way to the hairdresser. The officer made Lucy get out of the car and step onto the sidewalk for her safety while her partner stood in the road and signaled the other cars to go around Lucy's.

The young policewoman struck up a conversation with Lucy as they waited for the tow truck. She still hadn't recognized Lucy. Lucy wondered out loud how she would get to the hairdresser and the policewoman told her to get into the police car. She would take her. On the way, the two women chatted about the way Palm Springs had grown over the years and about the city's mayor, Sonny Bono.

When they pulled up in front of the beauty shop a few minutes later, Lucy took off her sunglasses as she said good-bye to the officer and it was only then that the girl recognized her.

"You're Lucy!"

Lucy took the girl's hand and said, "I thought you knew that. Isn't that why you drove me over here?"

"No," said the girl. "I just felt sorry for you."

Working was Lucy's favorite thing to do. Whenever she mentioned the word "work," it was soon followed by another word . . . "fun." For Lucy, they were the same thing. Aside from her children, Lucy's real joy in life was performing. In that sense, she never grew up. In an early acting class, I remembered a teacher who always said that children made the best actors because of their commitment to make-believe. Make-believe is the best kind of play there is for children. The limitations of a child are enlarged in direct proportion to his or her capacity to dream. As a child, Lucy was limited by few children to play with, so she made them up. As a teenager, she was confined to a hospital bed, so she dreamed of dancing on Broadway and gave herself the will to get up and do it.

The character of "Lucy" was a child. It was a pure distillation of one side of Lucy Ball herself. She was a many-faceted woman, but her writers captured the soul of the "kid." The "Lucy" character always wanted her own way, wasn't crazy about sharing, loved to make up wild schemes, pouted, whined, nagged, and was always getting into trouble.

Lucille Ball liked the "Lucy" character. "I found a character I wanted to play and loved doing, and had a chance to do it again and again and again and that's great. 'Lucy' never did anything to hurt anybody. She was bemused and . . . bewitched, bothered, and bewildered."

With *The Lucy Show* came a subtle but necessary change in her character. The element that had made *I Love Lucy* click in the first place was gone. Lucy and Ricky were no longer involved in a domestic comedy . . . there was no battle of the sexes. Lucy Carmichael was a widow. She had to be more responsible than Lucy Ricardo was, because she was the sole support of two children. At the same time, the "Lucy" character was "irresponsible." Adjustments had to be made, which meant change—the word Lucille hated more than any other.

Lucy had learned her lessons about how far she could take "Lucy"; what worked and didn't work. Even though Lucy Ricardo had the most famous baby in America, you didn't think of "Lucy" as being sexual. She and Ricky slept in separate beds, and never showed any more passion than the occasional hug and kiss. "Lucy" could be a seductress, but it was always funny. In an episode of *The Ann Sothern Show*, Lucy appeared as Lucy Ricardo in an overtly sexual story. Lucy was trying to make Ann fall for her boss and pretended to make a pass at him, thereby making Ann jealous.

Lucy didn't like the result. "The whole show seemed a little smarmy. It just wasn't right. I was still supposed to be married to Ricky and I'm throwing myself on another guy, and the audience just hated it and they let me know it, too." Lucy knew the bounds of the "Lucy" character, and no matter what characters around her changed, "Lucy" stayed the same.

Although Desi was gone from the show,

Lucy still had Vivian. She felt Vivian was her true equal, the Laurel to her Hardy, the Costello to her Abbott. Lucy liked to make an analogy comparing acting to badminton. To be a great player, you needed a great opponent; someone who could hit the bird back as forcefully and skillfully as you hit it to him. If you kept hitting the ball and the other player kept letting it drop, it would be pretty dull. After nine years together, Vivian could swat the birdie right back to Lucy and even ace her a few times in the process.

As president of Desilu, Lucy did not want to be considered a figurehead. She hired Oscar Katz, an old friend, to run the day-to-day business affairs of the studio, but gave every aspect of production her full creative input. Oscar recalled in a CBS interview with Dan Rather that "Lucy was very involved. We first met on the set of *My Favorite Husband*. When she didn't know how to do something, she learned."

He was right. She was asked to play the saxophone for a show and learned in a week. She was asked to learn to roller-skate for a show and became a crack skater in a week. She could certainly learn how to run a studio. Bob Schiller agreed. "It was amazing to see her do things better than the way you imag-

253

ined them. She never ad-libbed. She always wanted to know where she was supposed to be, and God help any actor who wasn't where *he* was supposed to be. She willed herself to do things. She was terrified of an elephant but willed herself to work with it. There was nothing she wouldn't try."

Lucy wanted to establish a personal relationship with every one of her employees on the lot, right down to the security guard. She was leaving the studio late one night when she stopped to say good night to the guard on duty. She didn't recognize him, and he told her he was new. He had just started the same day. She introduced herself, and he said, "It's nice to meet you, Miss Ball."

She said, "Call me Lucy!" She noticed he was shivering, and asked if he had a jacket. He said he didn't, but assured her that he was warm enough. He waved at her and wished her a good evening.

Lucy drove the car out into the street, made a wide U-turn, and headed back through the studio gate. A few minutes later, she drove through again and handed the guard a warm coat. "Now put that on, or you'll catch cold. And just leave it there in case you forget your coat again." She wasn't a studio chieftain—she was a den mother.

Lucy enjoyed the developmental side of producing. She liked to find new properties by good writers and match them up with her friends. She had done it with Ann Sothern, and wanted to do it for Ethel Merman.

In the early sixties, Merman quit Broadway. She was married to Bob Six, founder and president of Continental Airlines, and he was based in Denver. She had just finished several years on Broadway and touring *Gypsy,* and she didn't want another show. She wanted as normal a life as possible, and a series was nine-to-five work. Merman came to California to look around and called Lucy, who invited her to come over and join Vivian at her house, where they could do each other's hair. Vivian had been in several Broadway shows with Ethel, and knew her from the early thirties. The three "girls" sat around drinking Early Times bourbon one Sunday afternoon, and trying out different hairstyles on each other. Lucy wanted Ethel (Merman not Mertz) to become part of the Desilu stable. So did Merman.

Desilu offered several pilots to the network during the 1962–63 season; two of which were the Ethel Merman pilot and a

Glynis Johns pilot. Lucy loved the way Merman's show turned out. She was cast as a former Broadway singer who now owned a hotel in the South Seas. The arena gave her the opportunity to work opposite many guest stars who checked into the hotel for vacation, and it also gave her a chance to sing. Lucy thought it was surefire. The second pilot was called *Glynis*, and it was the story of a woman mystery writer who investigated crimes. Lucy hired her former *Wildcat* costar Keith Andes to play Glynis Johns's husband.

The Desilu shows for that year were sent to CBS for its consideration. Lucy believed in loyalty, and since CBS had given her and Desi their chance, she always sent that network her shows first. She talked to Bill Paley, who said he liked most of the material he'd seen but he only had room for one show and it was between Ethel and Glynis. Lucy begged him to take the Merman show, but Paley thought the Glynis Johns show was better, and opted for it. Lucy was very disappointed. She didn't think the public would take to Glynis Johns week after week, and she was right. After three months, the show was pulled.

Lucy gave Merman a consolation prize by giving her a guest starring role in a two-part

Lucy Show. She came on as Ethel Merman who was disguising herself as Agnes (Merman's mother's name) Schmidlapp to keep a low profile in the community. In part one, Lucy teaches the Merm how to sing and project loudly, and in episode two, they do a Roaring Twenties show for the PTA. Lucy laughed when she thought about Merman. "She was one of a kind. We used to go to a Chinese restaurant after rehearsals with the boys and Ethel. There were about twelve of us. We all ordered different things except Ethel, who ordered one dish and announced, 'I don't share!'"

Lucy liked to fill every minute of the day. When she had time off from work, she filled it with work. She was attracted to two big screen projects. Lucy enjoyed her television series because it was like doing a play every week and Lucy loved the theater. She also liked the movies because film was her background and she enjoyed acting for the camera. "It's a whole different set of muscles."

Lucy almost went back to Broadway. David Merrick came to see her. Lucy pointed to the spot on the sofa where he sat. "He asked me to replace Carol Channing in *Hello, Dolly!*," Lucy said. "I saw the show and Carol was great and I said yes. I'd love to do it—on one condition. I told him I would do the show on Broadway *if* he promised me the movie. He said he couldn't do it, and I said no. Just as well. It was a lousy picture anyway."

During a break from shooting *The Lucy Show*, Lucy took Gary and the kids to New York, where the World's Fair was honoring her with Lucille Ball Day. The crowds were massive, equal to the number Pope Paul VI saw on his New York trip the following year.

Lucy wanted to work through her summer hiatus from the show and signed to appear in *Critic's Choice* with Bob Hope. Hope was the motivating factor in doing the film. She loved performing with him. He was truly her equal in the "badminton" game of acting. The script was an inside show-business joke based on the lives of the playwright Jean Kerr *(Mary, Mary)* and her drama-critic husband, Walter Kerr *(The New York Times)*. Lucy writes a play that gets produced, and Bob has to review it. What might have been a funny Carol Burnett sketch turned into a tedious and unfunny film.

The next summer hiatus, Lucy tried to mix vacation and work together. *Lucy in London* was a one-hour special filmed in the British capital. Lucy appeared as Lucy Carmichael, who had won a first-class vacation in London, including her very own guide and Rolls-Royce. The guide was Anthony Newley, and the Rolls-Royce was a motorcycle and a sidecar. The script by Pat McCormick was uneven, but Lucy had fun.

Lucy had a good laugh before she started shooting early one morning. She was playing Anne Boleyn walking along the Thames in a scene that required them to begin at five in the morning. Lucy couldn't understand why they had to start shooting so early. Between having to do her hair and makeup, and getting into a huge Elizabethan costume, she would have to get up at three in the morning to start shooting by five. She went to the production manager and asked him what the deal was.

He explained to Lucy that the only place she could make her costume change was the house that Anne Boleyn lived in. It housed the only bathroom along their section of the river. The problem was that the man who lived there was an early riser and wouldn't let anyone use the house after he arose at 5:00 A.M.

Lucy went to see him and found him to be a delightful but very old and somewhat blind country gentleman, who was more set in his ways than she was. He welcomed her using his bathroom and guest room, but he wanted no one in the house when he awoke.

On the day of the shoot, Lucy dragged herself out of bed at three in the morning and waited for Hal King to do her makeup and Irma Kusely to do her hair. They were finished by four-thirty, and Lucy told them to leave so that she could put on her Anne Boleyn costume. "The skirt was so full that it brushed the sides of the tiny hallways in the little house, and it was so long it made me look like I didn't have any feet. It looked like I was floating."

Just as Lucy finished dressing and was looking herself over in the long mirror, she noticed that she was still wearing her watch and that it was 5:00 A.M. She quickly took off the watch and tried to get out before the old man got up. As she turned the corner of the hallway, the squire's door opened and he stepped out. Lucy was too far along to stop, so she just kept gliding along. She could see the old man gasp and his eyes pop out as he saw the ghost of Anne Boleyn float past him and disappear out the door.

During the third season of *The Lucy Show*, Vivian Vance gave Lucy the news she knew was coming but didn't want to hear. Vivian didn't want to play anymore. She wanted to go home to her husband in Connecticut and stay there. She had a new marriage, and it couldn't work if she and her husband never saw each other. Thinking back to the days when she and Desi were separated during their first years of marriage, Lucy couldn't have been more understanding.

Lucy still had a fine playmate in her old friend Gale Gordon. "He was great. He'd do anything. He was such a good sport." She would soon add two more playmates to the show—Little Lucie and Desi, Jr. At last Lucy felt they were ready.

CHAPTER
Eighteen

IN JANUARY OF 1989, I asked Lucy to go to an AIDS benefit show with me at the Variety Arts Theatre in downtown L.A. She was reluctant to make the long trip from Beverly Hills until I told her the show was starring one of her favorite performers, Lucie Arnaz. She accepted immediately. She loved to watch Lucie perform.

The next day, Lucie called her mother, told her about the event, and said she had

261

reserved a ticket for her. Since I had my own set of tickets, we decided we'd go together, but we wouldn't sit together.

A week before we went to see the show, Lucy was getting very excited about a night on the town. Gary didn't like to go out, so I was more than happy to take Lucy wherever she wanted. As we started playing backgammon, she started planning. It was like a "Lucy" scheme from one of her old scripts.

LUCY: Okay. Here's what we'll do.

JIM: About what?

LUCY: About tomorrow night. Did you forget?

JIM: About what?

LUCY: Now stop it. You and I are going to see Lucie.

JIM: Lucy who?

LUCY: Come on now. I'm going to drive with her to the theater and . . .

JIM: You're going to drive with somebody else.

LUCY: Right.

JIM: And you're going to sit with somebody else.

LUCY: Right.

JIM: Then how can we be going together?

LUCY: Well, we are. Now we'll meet at the theater at five-thirty and—

JIM:: But the show doesn't start until eight.

LUCY: (LOOKING AT JIM AS IF HE'S CRAZY) So?

JIM: What should we do for two and a half hours?

LUCY: Why can't we get something to eat?

JIM: We could, except that the only restaurant around that section of town is a dingy little coffee shop.

LUCY: (LOOKING AT OLD CRAZY JIM AGAIN) So? What's the matter with dingy old coffee shops?

JIM: They're fine. Except for when you have to eat in them.

LUCY: Well, it's the only place around there. Do you want to have dinner or not?

JIM: Well, let's see. The alternative is to stand on the street corner in the cold and look for out-of-state license plates.

LUCY: So?

JIM: (LOOKING AT LUCY AS IF SHE'S THE CRAZY ONE) Let's have dinner.

As the day of the performance approached, Lucy checked and rechecked our plans. She wanted to make a schedule and stick to it. I told her three friends of mine, CBS executive Anthony Barnao, producer Eleanor Albano, and our mutual friend Steve Schalchlin, would join us for dinner at the coffee shop. Lucy was very agreeable. She liked to have a large group around the dinner table.

Right on time, Steve and I arrived at the Variety Arts Theatre and found the lobby deserted. Unlike New York, which is alive and kicking twenty-four hours a day, the downtown section of Los Angeles becomes a ghost town at five o'clock. We opened the theater doors and saw people scurrying with ladders and pieces of scenery. I ran into my old friend David Galligan, who directed the show, and before I could say, "Have you seen Lucy?," he said, "She just went downstairs."

The basement of the Variety Arts Theatre was a set from a gothic horror movie: large, damp granite-block walls lighted by dim, naked white bulbs and pocked with a catacomb of dressing rooms. I could hear her voice coming from the darkness somewhere in front of me: "Jesus! How the hell do you get out of here?"

We searched for the voice and found Lucy and Lucie standing in front of a dirty white sheet that gave some privacy to a makeshift dressing area. Lucie Arnaz looked at us and said, "Ain't show biz glamorous?" Lucy looked sensational. She was all in black. Black slacks and shoes, black turtleneck shirt, black leather jacket, and diamonds for days. Lucy and Lucie were talking to Lucie's (and the show's) musical director, Ron Abel.

Ron and I have known each other for almost twenty years. I knew his family in Westchester. Ronnie is a very impressive-looking man: tall, fit, with alabasterlike white skin and a mane of blond hair that extends to his waist. Lucy kissed Ron as we left and said, "Say hello to your mother for me." With that, they both broke out laughing.

Ron and Lucy had a private joke about Ron's mother, Pearl, a nice Jewish lady from Scarsdale. For years, Lucy thought that Pearl was a large black woman. It was all a case of mistaken identity. After the opening of an engagement in Atlantic City, the producers gave Lucie a party for a thousand people. Lucy ran into Ron Abel in the crowd and told him she wanted to meet his mother; where was she? Ron looked around the room and spotted her on the balcony wearing a purple dress. He pointed her out to Lucy and left to fetch her so he could introduce them. Lucy looked where Ron was pointing, but before she found the spot, Pearl traded places with a large black woman in a purple dress. When the black lady saw Lucy staring up at her, she waved. Lucy assumed that it was Ron's mother, and left the party before she could meet the real Pearl Abel.

The joke was exposed a few years later when Lucy and Ron were talking and she wondered if she could ask him a personal question: How did he get such fair coloring with one black parent? Every time Lucy and I went out and we passed a large black lady, I'd nudge her and say, "Is that Ron Abel's mother?"

The coffee shop I referred to before is actually one of Los Angeles's famous eateries called the Pantry. The Pantry is a no-decor, no-tablecloths, no-checks-or-credit-cards, no-reservations, no-manners, no-nonsense, no-frills chophouse. You wait on a long line in the street until a table is ready, and your party must be complete before you are seated.

Lucy, Steve, and I walked across the street and up to the front door. There was a table for six, but only three of us were there. Anthony and Eleanor were late, and I wondered if they would make Lucille Ball stand outside while the rest of the party showed up.

When we walked in the front door, the manager looked up and saw Lucy right away. He looked like a Warner Bros. cartoon character whose eyes fly out of his head, bounce off one wall, then another, then rocket back into their sockets. An audible rumble of customers mumbling to each other about who had just walked in the front door made us feel as if we'd been through a minor earthquake.

The manager picked up three menus and walked up to us as proudly as the maître d' at Sardi's. "Good evening! How many in your party?"

"Five," I said, "but the other two . . ."

"Right 'dis way," he chirped in a thick Spanish accent.

We walked two steps to the large table in the middle of the room. It was a few feet from a wall-to-wall picture window that faced the street. He gave us each a menu and backed away from the table, gliding and bowing his way back to the cash register. Lucy had turned a coffee shop into a café.

The waitress put plates of coleslaw in front of us, pointed to the specials listed on the blackboard over the counter, did a little curtsy, and also backed away. It was fascinating to look out the window and watch the reaction of those people passing by who turned to see Lucille Ball sitting in the most unlikely spot in the world.

Lucy didn't want to order until Anthony and Eleanor got there, but they were over an hour late and we were getting restless. She had been telling stories and picking on her coleslaw and signing autographs when the manager came up to the table. He was very apologetic. "I forgot to tell you. Your friends called. They will be late. They will meet you at the show."

I was relieved. Now, we could order. I asked Lucy, "What do you want?"

"Nothing," she said with a little burp. "I'm too filled with coleslaw."

I wanted to tell her, "No eats, no seats!"

After coleslaw, we walked back to the theater and met Anthony, who ran toward us, laughing. He was red in the face and could hardly breathe, laughing and trying to talk at the same time.

"What's so funny?" We were all starting to laugh just from the infectiousness of it.

"The Pantry! I called to say I'd be late. Did you get the message?" We told him we had.

"Because when I called, a man with a Spanish accent answered, and I told him I wanted to leave a message for one of the customers. The guy said, 'We don't take no messages,' and started to hang up. I yelled, 'Wait! Wait! Wait! It's important I talk to this guy.' The manager said, 'Well, how will I know who this guy is?' and I said, 'It's easy. He's sitting with Lucille Ball.' Then there was a long pause, and finally the guy said, 'He's with who?'

"I said, 'Lucille Ball.' Then there was another pause and he said real sarcastically, 'And who's this? Ricky Ricardo?'" The four of us almost fell down laughing. Lucy was still laughing when we walked into the lobby of the theater.

That now-familiar rumble that goes through a room when Lucy enters passed around us like a wave. A spotlight from a TV camera blinded Lucy and knocked her a little off balance. A reporter from *Entertainment Tonight* asked her what she was doing there.

She said, "I know a lot of people who are performing here, including my daughter, and I wouldn't miss it for anything. But for Jerry Herman especially . . . and the same reason everyone is interested . . . a very worthwhile cause."

Lucie was terrific that night. Her mother was very proud that her daughter could sing, since she couldn't. She wondered where the talent came from, because she once admitted that she thought Desi's singing had "more volume than tone." Little Lucie knew how to please a crowd . . . she learned at the feet of the master.

Both kids had wanted to "get in the act" from the time they were very young. They followed in their mother and father's footsteps with their "Garage Follies," and were frustrated by watching other children play their mother's children on her series. Every year they asked to be on the show, and every year Lucy said no. She surprised all of them when she finally said yes.

If her children were going to be in show business, she wanted them to learn the business the right way. She knew there could be a "curse" on stars' children who wanted to go into the industry, having fame before they had the basics. When Lucy was convinced that her children would soon be looking for work, she decided to hire them herself.

Lucy believed in "Do as I do, and don't pay any attention to what I say." She treated her children as she did any other coworker, and made the same demands of them that she did of any professional. She saw the potential in both of her children and set out to cultivate it. She was not a pushy stage mother.

Lucy loved to use guest stars on her show, and most celebrities jumped at the chance to appear with her. It was good for their image to be shown doing something different, and it was a good story device to see the Lucy character react to the famous.

Lucy had mixed experiences with some guest stars; she loved working with Carol Burnett and Patti Andrews but hated Rudy Vallee and Joan Crawford.

Lucy first saw Carol Burnett in *Once Upon a Mattress* and knew she would be a major star. Early in Carol's career, Lucy told her if she ever needed her for anything to call. In 1966, the call came. CBS was planning a variety "special" to star Carol Burnett. If the special was successful, it would become a regular series on the network. Carol asked for only two guest stars: Lucille Ball and

Zero Mostel. Lucy loved doing the show because she had a "good player" in Carol and was reunited with Zero, with whom she had appeared in *DuBarry Was a Lady*.

In an interview, Carol Burnett marveled at Lucy's consummate knowledge about putting a show together: "Lucy saw it all. There were eyes in the back of her head. She knew the lights, the scenery, the costumes, the music, the makeup. Everything. And she was always right!"

Carol Plus Two was a show Lucy enjoyed watching again and again. It contained two of her all-time favorite sketches. One sketch had Lucy and Carol as two scrubwomen on the midnight shift at the William Morris Agency. They put million-dollar deals together as they emptied wastepaper baskets, and sang a duet with dueling mops called "Chutzpah!"

The other sketch was called "Good-bye, Baby!" Lucy, on her way to catch a bus for her first vacation in twenty years, is saying good-bye to her sister (Carol) and her eight-month-old nephew. Carol won't let Lucy leave until the baby says good-bye.

Lucy stands over the carriage egging the child on, repeating over and over, "Good-bye, baby!" with no response from the precocious little brat. Finally, the kid "goo-goos" a good-bye after Lucy bribes him with her plane ticket to Miami and five hundred dollars in cash. Several times during the scene, Carol Burnett is obviously biting her lip to keep from bursting out laughing at Lucy's antics.

After Lucy and I watched this sketch, we always closed our telephone conversations or afternoons with a twangy, nasal "Good-bye, baby!" to each other.

Carol Plus Two was a huge hit. The show became the series that ran on CBS for the next eleven years. Lucy had Carol on her show many times and really enjoyed a two-part episode featuring Carol and Lucy in stewardess school. She would have Carol on the show as often as possible. The same was not true for other performers.

Lucy had always wanted to work with stars she had idolized. One was Rudy Vallee, and the other was Joan Crawford.

For Vallee, the writers came up with a Roaring Twenties idea that could include his megaphone crooning and end with a big Charleston. Lucy had looked forward to the week with Vallee, but couldn't wait until it was over. "He was one of the most obnoxious men I've ever met. Wildly egotistical and totally foul-mouthed. He was supposed to make an entrance from behind a door, and all you could hear all over the place was, 'Fuck this! And fuck that!,' and God knows what else. He talked that way so much, I don't think he knew how offensive he was. When I told him to shut up, that he was being offensive in front of the kids, he actually looked surprised."

Lucy was wary of having Joan Crawford as a guest. She had heard rumors about Crawford's toughness and ego and hard drinking; probably the same things Crawford had heard about Lucy. When I told Lucy that my father had an affair with Joan Crawford in 1960–61, Lucy was very interested. When I told her I had remained friends with Crawford up to her death in 1977, she wanted to hear every word.

The first time I ever met the great Joan Crawford, she was in a dressing gown dyeing her hair red. Lucy's eyes popped out. "In a dressing gown . . . were you having an affair with her, too?"

I told her that I traveled to South America on the S S *Brasil* with my father in the summer of 1960. Shortly after the ship sailed, we heard there were several celebrities on board, including *The New York Times* caricaturist Al Hirschfeld, financier Louis Wolfson, and the great Joan Crawford. I was going on fourteen and didn't know who Joan Crawford was, but my handsome widower father set about to meet her. He asked everyone on the social staff if they had seen her, knew her cabin number, what activities she liked, or when she might be around.

On the first morning at sea, I met two nice girls my own age named Cindy and Cathy. We took to each other at once, and after lunch they invited me down to their cabin to play a game of Monopoly and meet their mother.

I went down and was introduced to their mother, Joan. She was sitting at her mirrored dressing table and was very nice and very friendly. She didn't mind having a young man in the room as she worked on her hair. As we talked, we all laughed and joked. It was a very easy atmosphere. I still had no idea this was the famous star everyone was dying to meet.

Later that evening, as my father and I sat down to dinner, I told him I was anxious to introduce him to the mother of my new friends, Cindy and Cathy. Always the matchmaker, I mentioned that she was very beautiful and very single. He wasn't interested. He didn't want to meet any women who were the marrying kind.

A few minutes into our dinner, we heard applause coming from the entrance to the dining room. The applause started rolling through the room like a wave growing louder. My father gaped when he spotted her.

"That's Joan Crawford. That's her!"

When Joan saw me, she swept over to the table and kissed me on each cheek. "Jimmy, dear, it's so good to see you again. This must be your charming father. Hello, Pete."

My father was as speechless as Ralph Kramden in a spotlight. Joan continued, "Peter, I'd like you to meet my daughters, Cindy and Cathy." My father shook their hands and babbled out a hello. Joan started for her table and looked back over her shoulder as she went, "Let's have a drink together later, shall we?"

My father's affair with Joan was more than a shipboard romance and less than a relationship. After a year, they saw each other as friends, and after two years they didn't see each other at all. I continued seeing Joan. We would correspond frequently, meet for lunch or dinner, or sometimes I would go up to her apartment on Fifth Avenue and talk.

I told Lucy about one night in particular that I thought I got an insight into Joan. Whenever I went to her apartment, she always greeted me as if she were about to have her portrait painted. One Saturday night, I called her and asked if she felt like company. She told me to come over. When I got off the elevator (which opened into her apartment), I saw a lady standing in front of me dressed in an old bathrobe, turban, and no makeup. I asked if Miss Crawford was home, and Joan looked at me and said, "I don't look that bad, do I?"

We went into the kitchen, where she was cooking bouillabaisse for a dinner party the next night. She apologized for her appearance, but added she felt comfortable enough with me that she didn't have to perform. She shook her head sadly and said, "It's a production to go for a stick of gum."

She looked at me directly, and took a drag of her cigarette. Although she was not drunk, I could tell she had been drinking. There was no pretense about her at that moment. She said, "Whenever I go out that door, I have to be Joan Crawford. I can't go out without every hair in place or without my makeup and a good dress."

"Why not?" I wanted to know.

She banged her hand on the counter. "Because people expect Joan Crawford, and that's what I have to give them."

As the evening progressed with Crawford, she drank heavily. I told her how much I wanted to be an actor, and I asked her advice about what I should do. Like Sadie Thompson in the last scene of *Rain*, where she feels sorry for everyone in the whole damn world, complete with a shaft of light across her face, she said, "Who knows what you should do? Who knows what anyone should do? I didn't want to be an actress. I wanted to be a star. And I always knew I'd be a star as long as my back held out." I didn't understand at that moment what she meant, but a few years later it dawned on me that she wasn't talking about hard work.

Lucy interrupted me and asked if I had ever heard about the famous House of Stars in the Hollywood Hills? I hadn't. She told me in the thirties and forties, there was a house of ill-repute where the prostitutes were made to look like the most famous movie stars of the day. A customer would come in and ask for Mae West or Myrna Loy or Joan

Crawford, and for a very large amount of money, was bedded with the star's lookalike. Lucy looked around the room checking for intruders before she added, "I always heard that the Joan Crawford girl looked so much like Crawford that everyone thought it was Crawford."

I leaned in to keep things confidential. "Do you think it was?"

"No," roared Lucy. "She'd have to be in makeup at six A.M. You can't screw around when you're under contract."

I asked Lucy how the experience of working with Crawford had been. She told me she fired her after the first rehearsal. "She was drunk. She showed up at ten o'clock in the morning for the first read-through, and she was bombed. She was drinking straight vodka from this silver flask, and she was drinking it in front of the kids. She was saying all the words, but it was like she was a robot. About lunchtime, Joan passed out cold, and that did it. As soon as she woke up, I fired her."

Herb Kenwith, the show's director and an old friend of Crawford's, begged Lucy to give her another chance. Crawford, after her revival, said the heat had gotten to her. Lucy gave her another chance, and Crawford did finish the show. Lucy admitted it was one of the worst.

Lucy enjoyed working with the Burtons during *Here's Lucy,* although in his published diaries, Burton revealed he didn't feel the same way.

When *The Diaries of Richard Burton* were published in early 1989, those of us around Lucy tried very hard to keep the book from her. We read that Burton took her over the coals, and indeed he even went so far as to say, "I loathe Lucy." Lucy got hold of the book despite our efforts and read about the bitter feelings Burton had for her. "I can't understand it," she said through her tears. "I thought he liked me."

Gary and Lucy were at a party in 1969 when Burton asked her if he and Elizabeth could make a guest appearance on the show. She asked when they were available, he said now, and she called the writers to have a script drafted immediately. The plot centered around the famous sixty-nine-carat diamond ring Richard had given Elizabeth as a present.

I asked her if they had any problems on the set, and she told me about one incident that could have elicited Burton's wrath. At one point in the plot, Burton is evading the

280

press by disguising himself as a plumber. Lucy (in desperate need of a plumber) runs into Burton and asks if he is free. In his grandest Shakespearean voice, Burton answered, "What man is ever free?"

According to Lucy, Burton was losing a lot of laughs because he was mumbling his lines. The director was too intimidated by Burton to tell him to speak up, so producer Lucy shouldered the responsibility of telling the great actor herself.

She went to Burton's dressing room and told him that there were at least eleven laughs in the scene, and he was losing most of them because he couldn't be heard. Burton was very polite and told her that he would speak up. During the next run-through, Burton *screamed* the lines at the top of his lungs, which embarrassed and hurt Lucy. "I was only trying to help him."

At the taping of the show, Burton delivered his lines audibly, and the result was sixteen laughs where everyone thought there were only eleven. Lucy shook her head as she remembered the incident. "I just don't understand why he would say those things about me. He even came back after that and did us a favor. Oh well!"

By 1966, Lucy was getting weary of wearing many different hats. She didn't enjoy the duties she had as president of the studio. She didn't like the business end of it. She cried for days before the annual stockholders' meeting, she cried during the meeting, and would cry for several days afterward. She never fired anyone except for the most egregious and repeated offenses, and cried when she had to do that. The business end of it was too grown up for her, and she didn't want to handle it.

She loved the artistic side of her duties as president, because it gave her a chance to be creative and to give others the chance to create. Desilu had done well with her as president, and was developing several new shows, including one called *Star Trek*.

Gulf and Western came to Lucy with an offer to buy her out for three times what she had paid only seven years before. She would get $17 million for her shares in Desilu. The thought of it made Lucy cry again. "Boy, did I cry over that one."

She agreed to sell only after a face-to-face meeting with Charles Bludhorn, CEO of Gulf-Western. She liked him and believed that he would treat the employees kindly. She made sure everyone's job was secure. Still, she cried.

There was symbolism in the sale of Desilu. Lucy and Desi had been married to other people for over five years, but Lucy found it hard to let go of Desi. When she sold the Desilu studios, it was a final act of saying good-bye, because for Lucille Ball the word "Desilu" never meant the studio, it meant the ranch in the Valley, the home she had shared with Desi for fifteen years.

CHAPTER
Nineteen

LUCY LOVED TO take a walk in the morning. She would stroll up Roxbury Drive on Gary's arm, past the houses where her friends Aggie Moorehead, Oscar Levant, Lionel Barrymore, and Jeanne Crain once lived, and remember what things used to be like. Jack Benny lived next door to Lucy for years, and Jack would often drop in for a drink when his wife wasn't looking.

Lucy adored Jack Benny. She loved him as a performer, as a neighbor, and as a friend. "Jack would stop by every few days and have a drink with Gary. I would open the back door and hear them laughing when I walked in. It's great to come home to a house full of laughter." Lucy didn't share her warm feelings for Jack with his wife, Mary Livingston. Lucy out-and-out didn't like her.

It was painful for Lucy when Jack Benny moved out of 1002 North Roxbury a few years before his death in 1974. When she asked Jack why he had put the house up for sale, he shrugged and told her, "Mary thinks it would be best." Lucy was astonished. She knew that Jack loved that home and wanted to die there. The house was paid off, and the Bennys certainly didn't need the money. Lucy's theory was that Mary put the house on the market "just to be mean."

To say that Lucy thought Mary Livingston was a manipulative woman would be an understatement. Although they never had a fight or even raised their voices at each other, the tension level would increase several points when Lucy and Mary were in the same room. Lucy felt that Mary controlled Jack in much the same way Svengali controlled Trilby.

When Jack invited Lucy and Gary to see their new condo, Lucy waited for a time when she knew Mary would be out of town. Lucy walked into the apartment and could sense Jack's unhappiness, although he was trying to be cheerful about the spacious rooms and the wonderful view.

Jack took Lucy on a tour of the place, pointing out all the modern conveniences. When he got to the master suite, he peeked in and said, "This is Mary's bedroom." Lucy asked Jack where *his* bedroom was? Jack walked her down a long hallway and pointed to a small room off the kitchen. Lucy said, "It had a small single bed in the corner and a table next to it. There was no door to separate the room from the kitchen, just an open doorway. Like something a monk would live in."

Lucy was aghast, and asked Jack, "Where's the door? You don't have a door."

"No," Jack said. "I guess that's the way they're making them nowadays."

Lucy felt her blood pressure go up. "Jack, this is the maid's room."

"No," Jack said, "it's my room. It's perfectly fine."

Lucy persisted. "It's *not* fine. You have no privacy. You have no bathroom. Why are you sleeping back here in this little room?"

Jack said, "Well, Mary thinks it would be best."

When Lucy took her walks in the morning, all she saw as she walked around Beverly

Hills was what had changed. To herself, Lucy was just another person walking down the street, but I would see cars swerve nearly out of control when the driver recognized the pedestrian as Lucille Ball. One day, as she was walking up Rodeo Drive after getting her nails done, she turned around when the driver of a car started honking his horn repeatedly. He rolled down the window, stuck out his head, and yelled, "So, you're still working the streets, huh?" With that, he drove off in a huff, leaving Lucy laughing her head off. It was comedian Jay Leno.

Lucy walked where she was going whenever she could because she felt she was lucky to be able to walk at all. Lucy and I had a "metaphysical" conversation once about the years she spent as a paralyzed teenager. She would poo-poo me and laugh at my use of the word "metaphysical," but that's what it was. It started with a conversation about a book I gave Lucy that proposed *all* illness as psychosomatic. She believed that to a degree. She thought that headaches and high blood pressure and even heart problems could be self-originated, but not things like cancer or muscular dystrophy or AIDS.

She used her own paralysis as a teenager

to illustrate. "I didn't bring that on myself, did I?"

"Maybe you did."

"Why would I do that?"

We looked in the book, more for a laugh than anything else, and found the theory: Any kind of paralysis resulted from being "so scared that you can't move." Lucy got very serious when I read that. She thought about the two years she had spent in bed and tried to put it into perspective. When Lucy was struck, she was a sixteen-year-old girl alone in New York, five hundred miles from her mother, being told by everyone that she had no talent for the thing she wanted more than anything else in the world. A girl with Lucy's ego couldn't go home to her mother and say I failed—but she could go home if she was gravely ill.

Lucy said, "You know, I *was* so scared then. Maybe there's something to it." Then, shaking off any insights she might have had, she added, "What difference does it make? I got out of bed, didn't I? Here! Feel that!"

She was rubbing a spot on her right leg. I reached over and felt a large bump. "Does it hurt?"

"No, not at all. It's just a bump. That's

where they put the pins when I broke my leg."

Lucy always said she broke her leg, but actually another skier broke it for her. Lucy thought the incident changed her life more than any other, because she couldn't do physical comedy with the same ease as she had before. Even when her leg was completely healed, it never gave her the same support. She felt inhibited to "let go," because she was afraid of falling and hurting herself again. The postaccident Lucy was a measured, careful character, and not the willing-to-try-anything daredevil she had once been.

In 1973, Lucy was at her house in Snowmass, Colorado, after a season of shooting *Here's Lucy* and before filming was set to begin on Lucy's next feature film, *Mame*. Lucy was looking forward to *Mame*. It was a multimillion-dollar big-screen musical, the likes of which hadn't been made since the heyday of MGM. She was looking forward to relaxing before she went back to work.

Lucy, a good skier, was standing still when the freak accident took place. She was watching the action from a vantage point along a ski trail when, according to Lucy, "A lady went out of control, hit my pole, and I screwed myself right into the ground. Just like a corkscrew."

The way her face contorted as she told the story made it seem as though she was reliving the pain. "I had four screws in my leg. Both bones were broken, and there was a butterfly spiral break at the top. As soon as I hit the ground, I knew it was serious, and all I could think of was whether it was a bad sprain or a bad break. I wanted it to be the one that would heal faster. They took me down in a big basket. I was screaming all the way. I never had such pain in my whole life. All I kept thinking was, How long would it take to heal? How long would it take to heal? And the pain. They wouldn't give me anything for the pain."

"Why?"

"Would you believe this? Because I had a hamburger. Yeah! A hamburger, fries, and a coke. I had to wait *nine hours* before they could operate or give me anything for the pain. When the girl with the anesthesia put the mask over my face, I grabbed her hands and kissed them like I was a junkie. I thought when I came out of the operation, it would be the end of the pain, but it was only the beginning."

When Lucy woke up, the cast was unbearable. She kept telling the doctors that the cast had been put on too high, but they told her she knew her business and they knew theirs—the cast was fine. Lucy broke the cast herself and made them give her a new one. When they put the second cast on too high, she broke that one, too.

The writers of *Here's Lucy* decided to incorporate Lucy's injury into the scripts, and it gave her an opportunity to use a wheelchair in new pieces of business. Lucy knew that her injury could not be incorporated into *Mame*, and feared she would lose the job. The picture had been scheduled for a five-month shoot, and even if her leg was fully back, would the producers believe she could get through a five-month shoot?

When Lucy's cast was removed, it was obvious the leg was traumatically damaged. She wore a leg brace to hobble around. She couldn't walk right, and the thought of dancing terrified her. She had tremendous doubts about whether she could pull off *Mame*.

Lucy kept waiting for the call that she had been fired, but instead came a call to say she was the only choice for Mame, and the others would wait for her. She asked who was going to choreograph the dances, and was told it was Onna White, who won the Oscar for

Oliver! and several Tonys for her work on Broadway.

Lucy called Onna to ask if they could get a head start because of her leg. Onna accepted enthusiastically and told Lucy that if she did everything that she told her, she would get her leg back in shape completely.

Lucy liked Onna immediately. She had found a match for herself. Onna is a no-nonsense professional with a great sense of humor who could smoke and drink Lucy under the backgammon table. After their first workout, Onna made a dinner of corned beef and cabbage soaked in Early Times bourbon, and their friendship was sealed for life. Lucy often said that if it hadn't been for Onna, she wouldn't have been able to walk without a limp.

Lucy was still wearing a brace months after the cast came off. Onna wanted Lucy to throw the brace away to strengthen her leg, but it was Lucy's security blanket, and she flatly refused. Onna was on her way to Lucy's house for their morning workout when she heard on the radio that Lucy had fallen and might have rebroken her leg. Onna put her foot to the pedal and sped down Laurel Canyon.

When she got to the house, Lucy's leg was

feeling sore but not broken. Lucy told Onna she lost her balance while trying to get something from the top of a closet and went "ass over teakettle." Onna was irate. She told Lucy to remove her brace at once. Lucy obeyed. Onna took the brace and burned it. They worked on the leg every day, and within a few weeks Lucy was kicking as high as any nineteen-year-old chorus girl.

Lucy wanted to thank Onna for her help and gave her a present—a fake fur coat. Onna put on the inexpensive coat to model it for Lucy, who thought it looked very stylish. Lucy admired the fake fur and said to Onna, "Well, that's stunning. Whatever did you wear before?"

Onna waited and delivered her reply as Vera would to Mame. "What did I wear before this? Mink!"

A broad smile crossed Lucy's face. She gave Onna a slight curtsy and said, "Touché."

Lucy got off to a bad start when the filming on *Mame* finally began. She had director approval and cast approval both stipulated in her contract, and she got neither. Gene Saks, who directed the Broadway show, was hired as director, and Madeline Kahn was cast as Agnes Gooch. Lucy didn't want either one of them.

She said, "I almost choked the day I heard they were signed. I should have said something, but I gave them the benefit of the doubt. They were both very respected in the business, and although I didn't know them personally, I thought, well, they couldn't louse things up too badly. Boy, was I wrong!"

At the time, Gene Saks was married to Lucy's costar, Beatrice Arthur. Lucy thought that Bea was one of the most gifted actresses around, and wanted to work with her. She thought if she got Saks fired, then Bea would follow behind him.

She disliked Madeline Kahn—right from the first moment she met her. Lucy talked about Kahn's "attempted" performance as Gooch through clenched teeth as we played one day. It was obvious she still had bitter feelings about her fifteen years after the fact.

Lucy hated what Kahn was doing to the character. She went to Gene Saks repeatedly, asking him to tell Kahn to start delivering Agnes Gooch. Lucy said, "Saks didn't do anything, or if he did, it had no effect. She was getting worse."

Lucy couldn't take it anymore and went

to Kahn herself. She said icily, "Excuse me, Madeline, but just when are we going to start seeing your interpretation of Gooch, dear?"

Kahn glared back at Lucy through a taut grin and said, "You *are* seeing her, dear!"

Lucy nodded and said, "Oh?," as if a great mystery of the universe had been revealed to her, and went back into the rehearsal room. She sweetly called Gene Saks out to join her privately for a moment. They walked out of the studio, and as soon as the door shut behind them, Lucy screamed into Saks's ear, "FIRE HER!" Saks fired her.

Lucy thought Kahn was being bad on purpose to get out of her contract—if she quit, she wouldn't be paid; if she was fired, she could collect her substantial salary and do what she wanted. Lucy wasn't surprised to learn Kahn started work on *Blazing Saddles* the day after she was fired from *Mame*.

Lucy didn't enjoy working on *Mame*, and she wasn't pleased with the result. She was afraid of hurting herself, and it took her focus away from building a character and acting it. Onna told me that before they would dance outside, Lucy would spend fifteen minutes walking up and down the lawn looking for gopher holes so she wouldn't fall.

Lucy didn't want Mame Dennis to be a

reincarnation of Lucy Ricardo, and turned to Gene Saks for help. She wanted him to *tell* her what to do, not no *ask* her. To her dying day, Lucy gave credit to Onna White for being the "spiritual" director of the picture.

At sixty-two, Lucy was starting to feel the wear and tear. She wasn't having fun anymore, and her bones ached whenever she tried anything strenuous. Her heart and her fans were telling her to stay, but her bones and her great sense of timing were telling her to "get off!"

Lucy called it a day with *Here's Lucy* in 1974, after a twenty-three-year run on network television. Her first few days at home, a retiree, were the most traumatic of her life. She thought about calling up the bosses and saying, "I was only kidding. I'll be right back," but didn't. She stood by her decision to "leave 'em beggin' for more."

CHAPTER
Twenty

ONNA WHITE HELPED bring Lucy and me together. I've known Onna for years, and after Lucy got my script, she called Onna to find out if I was an ax murderer or if she could safely spend an afternoon with me.

Onna called me one afternoon and invited me to a dinner party she was having for a few friends, including Gary and Lucy. Since I was spending the afternoon with Lucy, we decided to all go together. Lucy was looking forward to it because Onna was making her Early Times corned-beef-and-cabbage dinner.

Lucy had a wonderful time that night. She was in such a good mood that she insisted we sing a duet we had worked out together; Jim on tenor and Lucy on bass singing "I Don't Want a Ricochet Romance." Onna thought we sounded like Ethel Merman and Walter Brennan in heat. For dinner, ten of us sat around the table—Onna, Lucy, Gary, Gary's sister, Helen, Steve Schalchlin, director John Bowab, manager Bud Robinson, Lois Nettleton, Janis Paige, and myself. Lucy wore her hot-pink LUCY WHO? running suit, and was very relaxed. We laughed about whether we could get drunk from too much bourbon in the meat. Lucy spoke up, broadly slurring her words as she spoke: "Absolutely not! The bourbon burns up in the heat . . . damnit!" She ended with a big hiccup and brought the house down.

It made us laugh for two reasons. First, it was the greatest comedienne of the twentieth century performing for an audience of ten, and second, she didn't do it that often. Lucy was not a compulsive performer. She wasn't always "on." She wasn't always trying to be funny or to insert herself into situations. She would rather sit back and listen and ask questions and learn. So when she did come forth with the occasional inspired piece of shtick, we were surprised by it and we enjoyed it.

When Lucy decided to give up her weekly show, I think she *was* a compulsive performer. She had a lot of energy that needed to be channeled. By retiring, she was saying, "I will now only perform when *I* want." The problem was, she still wanted to do it all the time. Gary had golf, the kids had their own lives, Lucy had nothing to do, and it scared her. Lucy tried golf. She went out with Dinah Shore and did nothing but hit the ball into sand traps and roughs and gab with Dinah, and all the other players were yelling at them because they were holding everybody up. Lucy gave up golf after one try: "I hate it. It makes me too nervous."

She tried horseback riding, but it gave her pain in the broken leg. Her leg had limited her ability to enjoy physical activities. She needed a challenge. Lucy loved to play backgammon. After she retired, her love of the game turned into a mild obsession. There were backgammon tables in every part of the house. The pool house had two, in case a tournament erupted after a swim.

Lucy liked backgammon for a number of reasons. First, she was *playing with* somebody, and the better the player, the better the game. Two, it requires thought, skill, and talent. Three, it was exciting because winning depended on the right roll of the dice at the right time and a great deal of luck. Sound like show business?

Lee Tannen is a nephew of Gary Morton who befriended Lucy when he was eleven years old. Lucy and Lee were very close, and she loved to play backgammon with him. He's a great player, with an outstanding sense of humor. There were only laughs when Lee was around. Since Lee lives in New York, he became a little jealous of my relationship with Lucy. Lucy loved the rivalry. She would say little things to us about the other like a coquette who was playing one gentleman caller against the other beau. Lee called one day while I was there, and Lucy thought it was time to see if any fireworks would erupt between us on the phone. She thrust the phone at me and said, "Want to talk to Lee?"

I acted very uppity. "No, I don't."

With that, she said, "Here Lee. Say hello to Jim!"

I took the phone, and Lee said flatly, "Hello, Jim. Now, put Lucy back on!" I could hear the wink in his voice, and decided to play along. I growled into the phone, "Never call Miss Ball again!," and hung up. Lucy roared. She really loved that. Lee called back in a few minutes, and we all laughed.

I decided to take our imagined rivalry one step further. Lucy kept a framed picture of Lee on the small table in the backgammon corner. The day after our fake phone fight, I put a framed picture of myself right in front of Lee's.

A few weeks later, Lee came to the Coast, walked into the house, and immediately put his picture back in front. This became a running gag—whoever's picture was in front was the last one in the room.

When she retired, Lucy started going to Pip's, which was then a very popular backgammon club. Lucy would play with as many people as she could. She loved having new partners, and she loved having an audience.

She also filled the need for an audience by teaching. She loved having kids in front of her, and she believed in passing on the art of comedy even though she professed it couldn't be taught. She knew that only a handful of kids in a classroom of a hundred had the gift, and it was those few she was there for. The others in the class she came to entertain. Besides, she thrived on young people. She loved their spirit and their energy.

She laughed about the time she agreed to teach a class at Brandeis University. She told the staid dean that the classes would be question-and-answer. He asked her how she intended to formulate her final examination.

She looked at the dean. "You mean you want me to grade papers?"

The dean huffed, "Well, how else would you know if the student passed or failed?"

"I don't know," Lucy said. "Maybe we throw a pie in everybody's face, and whoever makes us laugh the most, we give the highest grade to."

Lucy's retirement also had an effect on her mother, DeDe. DeDe never missed a show in the twenty-three years Lucy was on the air. She would go wherever Lucy was to see her perform. DeDe saw her daughter go from a marginally talented, gawky teenager to one of the most beloved stars in the world.

In mid-1977, DeDe's health deteriorated quickly. She had a blood clot but still tried to stay active and get out of the house every day. DeDe kept her usual doctor's appointment on July 21, and the doctor found her in good shape for her eighty-five years. The next day, she felt a pain while getting ready to keep a lunch date with some friends. DeDe's nurse came in, and DeDe looked up at her and said, "This is it!," and died.

Her mother's death hit Lucy hard, although some people were shocked by her stoicism at the time. Lucy called the friends that DeDe was to meet that afternoon and said, "I'm sorry. My mother can't meet you for lunch today. She passed away this morning."

Lucy often looked at pictures of her mother and then would call in Frank Gorey. (Before he came to work for Lucy, Frank worked for DeDe as a driver and man around the house.) When Frank came in, Lucy would hold up a picture of DeDe and say, "She was a great gal, wasn't she, Frank?"

Frank would always answer very sincerely, "That she was, ma'am. That she was." Those who knew DeDe knew her as the last to leave a good party. If Lucy went over to see her mother and found she wasn't at home, she drove down the street to the local gin mill to find DeDe and Frank having a cocktail with some of the regulars. Lucy would walk in and say to her mother, "So here you are, Mom. I thought this was your night to go to San Pedro and pick up sailors."

Lucy had an idea for a television movie. She always wanted to work with Jackie Gleason, and when she read an article about Lillian Russell and "Diamond" Jim Brady, she thought it was a natural for them. Gleason agreed, but then they couldn't decide on a screenplay; then they couldn't coordinate their schedules or a location—Lucy wanted to shoot it in New York or L.A., but Gleason insisted on Florida. Little by little, the nitpicking eroded the enthusiasm they initially shared, and the project never materialized. Lucy regretted that she didn't try harder to work things out with Gleason and get *Lil 'n Jim* to the screen. In the meantime, she continued to make guest appearances on television, and definitely enjoyed doing some shows more than others.

She had two experiences she hated. She

agreed to be on Shirley MacLaine's special, *Gypsy in My Soul*. The premise of the show was a tribute to the chorus dancers who back up the star. Shirley became one of the dancers for the show, and Lucy was the only "star." Lucy's leg was killing her, but she didn't want to "play star" and ask for rest or any kind of special treatment. Shirley didn't give her any. "I was very hurt by the way Shirley treated me. It was like I wasn't there. She wasn't mean or anything like that, but, she wasn't friendly, either. I didn't know if I was doing good or bad. She just left me out in the cold." Lucy cocked her head and added, "And she was so good in *Terms of Endearment*. That's my favorite movie of all time."

Her most unpleasant experience was working with Mary Tyler Moore. Moore was doing a new series for CBS that was a musical-comedy series, a behind-the-scenes look at how a variety show is put together. The cast included pianist Stan Freeman and newcomers David Letterman and Michael Keaton. People on the staff of the show told me that Mary was sweet to Lucy, but Lucy didn't see it that way. She felt Mary didn't like her and was cold and aloof. Lucy complained, "I'd say something to her, and she'd smile that big, toothy smile and walk away."

Lucy had a number to sing in the show called "The Girlfriend of the Whirling Dervish." Lucy hated the song, and asked Mary to change it. She wouldn't. Lucy finally agreed to do the song, but clearly under protest. At the prerecording session, Lucy walked in ready for a fight. She told the director and the engineers that she would sing the number once and once only. If there was anything they had to work out technically, they should do it now, because she would do *one take and one take only!*

Lucy sang the song once through. After a beat, the sound engineer called out, "One more take, please!" Stan Freeman, who witnessed the incident, says that Lucy was like an out-of-control child. "She threw herself down on the floor kicking and screaming and yelling 'I won't! I won't! I won't!'" After she stopped screaming, she got up and did another take.

A few months before she died, I took Lucy to see a one-man show Stan Freeman was doing about the life of Oscar Levant. I told Lucy we were going to meet some other friends at the theater, and then go out for dinner afterward. She asked me whom we were meeting, and I told her one was cabaret star Charles Pierce, whom Lucy had seen in New York, and the other was "Dear Abby" herself, Abigail Van Buren.

"Oh, no!" Lucy said.

"What's the matter?"

"I can never tell them apart."

"Who can't you tell apart?"

"Abby and her twin sister, Ann Landers."

I said, "We're only going with one of them. You don't have to keep track of which one is which." That seemed to make sense to Lucy.

When we got to the theater, Charles Nelson Reilly, the show's director, met Lucy, Abby, and me at the curb and presented Lucy with a rose. Charles looked at Abby Van Buren and was flustered. No one had told him Abby was coming, and he didn't have a rose for her. He looked at Abby and said, "Somebody locked your rose in the box-office safe, but we've sent for a team of experts, and you'll have it by intermission." She did.

Although there was still only one of the twins with us, Lucy kept nudging me, saying, "Which one is she?"

I'd whisper, "Dear Abby!"

"Oh yeah. That's right."

It was fun to be with Lucy at intermission. People formed lines just to say hello and thank her for the laughs or just to say they loved her. Lucy was always gracious. She always asked them questions about themselves. Where were they from? What did they do? What were they interested in? She would correct anyone who came up to her and said, "Excuse me, Miss Ball . . ." with a "Please call me Lucy."

We went backstage to see Stan after the performance. Lucy raved about the show. Stan asked her if she remembered the day she recorded. "The Girlfriend of the Whirling Dervish," and she looked him with a blank stare and said, "Nope!"

When Bob Hope called, Lucy ran. He was one of her favorite partners. Lucy was ecstatic when Bob told her what he wanted her to do. The show was a tribute to vaudeville, and Bob wanted her to play Sophie Tucker and sing, "Some of These Days." They gave her a fat suit to wear under a spangled gown. She would watch the four-minute piece from time to time when she needed a laugh, and always said, "God, that was fun."

Lucy, after five years in retirement, had a wish that she wanted to make come true. She wanted to work with Vivian Vance once again. Vivian had been living in Connecticut with her second husband and was ill. She had suffered a stroke. After Vivian had had a few months of physical therapy, Lucy convinced her to come back to Hollywood and make one more show with her. Vivian agreed.

Lucy got as much of the old team together as she could. The writers came up with an idea: Lucy and Viv write a letter to President Carter and invite him to stay over at their house (as he was wont to do) during a forthcoming visit to their town.

I went to watch the taping, and when Vivian was introduced, the audience went wild. She came out and bowed and said she was happy to be back in town. This got another hand. It was obvious that she was still suffering the effects of the stroke. The left side of her face was partially paralyzed. It drooped noticeably.

Lucy was introduced and got a bigger hand than Vivian. The two of them gave each other a kiss, and the taping began. Lucy cried on her first entrance. She told the audience that this was the first show she had done since her mother's death, and it was difficult for her to know that DeDe wasn't out front. Lucy started again, and was letter-perfect. Vivian always stood stage right and was photographed only from the right side. It worked. The show was a hoot, and no matter what character names they were using, "Lucy" and "Ethel" were back together. I felt privileged to be watching the reunion. It was their only one.

Lucy hoped that she and Vivian could do a special a year. Vivian loved the idea—working once a year with Lucy suited her fine. It wasn't to be. Vivian died of cancer on August 17, 1979. Lucy was shattered. Her series, her mother, and her best buddy were all gone. Lucy had nobody to play with.

CHAPTER
Twenty One

I CAME HOME from shopping one morning and found a message on my answering machine. It was Lucy. She sounded like an irate customer calling the complaint department and finding it closed. "Yes, I do have a message, and I am leaving it at the sound of the beep. This is Thursday morning at five minutes of ten, and you should be up and out of bed. I've made my bed and I've done the dishes and I've taken my walk and I was thinking what the hell am I going to do for the rest of the day until Jim gets here . . . damnit. Good-bye, baby!" I called her back. She was in a very playful mood, and asked if I could come over at once. I said, "Only if you feed me."

When I got there, Roza had made chicken sandwiches for the two of us the way Lucy liked them, two *thin* pieces of bread with one *thin* slice of chicken with a mist of mayonnaise and cut into quarters. It was the smallest sandwich I had ever seen. Lucy started to laugh because I just sat there staring at it.

"This is lunch?"

"Yeah," she said. "Just leave whatever you can't eat."

She broke herself up, but I kept a straight face. I looked back down at the four tiny pieces of sandwich. "I have cuff links bigger than this." I took all four pieces, piled them on top of each other, put them in my mouth at one time, and tried to chew. Lucy was waving her hand, yelling, "Stop that! Stop that! You'll choke." I swallowed them with a gulp and asked her, "Where's lunch?"

Five months after her minor stroke in May of 1988, she was asked to appear on an all-star edition of the game show *Super Password*. The other players would be Betty

White, Carol Channing, and Dick Martin. I told Lucy we should play *Password* for a few days to get her back in the swing of things. Lucy loved the idea, and asked nurse Trudi and Frank Gorey to be the other team. Whenever Lucy looked at a new word, her eyes went around in their sockets. "God, I hope they're not as tough as these."

Password was the last major television appearance she made before the Oscars. She didn't enjoy doing guest shots, because she didn't like the way she looked. She said yes to *Password* for a few reasons; it would be fun, she would be seeing three old friends whom she enjoyed playing games with, and she wouldn't have to memorize any lines or learn any blocking. Most important, she would be in front of an audience.

The five shows were taped on September 24, 1988, a Saturday. Lucy tired easily, and wondered if she'd get through the very long day. But when Gene Wood announced her name, the studio audience stood as one and cheered for several minutes. You could almost see the energy pour into her and raise her up. When the ovation quieted, Betty White turned to the host, Bert Convy, and said, "Lucy who? I didn't get her last name." Lucy was having such a good time, she looked at the audience and said, "We're having more fun than they are."

When Lucy finished taping the fifth show seven hours later, she was exhausted. Whenever she performed, her energy level started in "high gear" and then switched into "overdrive." The stroke left Lucy hardly able to shift from second to third. It angered her that her body was giving up. Ann Sothern called her to suggest they do a movie together, but Lucy said no before the words were out of Ann's mouth. She told Ann that the public didn't want to see them looking the way they did, and besides, she didn't have the "oomph" anymore.

She had very bad memories of her most recent work. Whatever project she tried in the eighties backfired on her. She still blamed most of her physical troubles on becoming dehydrated during the filming of *Stone Pillow*. One of the reasons she accepted the part of the bag lady, aside from being a closet dramatic actress, was because she could look terrible and not care.

Once she was on the set, the shooting schedule was torture. Her right leg ached, her "friggin' shoulder" spasmed out of control, and she couldn't eat because of the 90-degree heat. Every muscle in her body ached. She recalls that she had only one laugh during the whole course of shooting.

Lucy was filming a scene that she likened to Snow White going through the forest where the trees grabbed her; a very scary sequence in which Florabelle escapes from a homeless shelter on a dark Brooklyn street. As she makes her way down the alley, she comes to a wall and looks over to see she is inches away from a nest of rats. She screams. Lucy began the scene somewhat squeamish, knowing there were going to be live rats so close to her. She said, "I started down the alley, got to the wall, took a deep breath, peeked my head over . . . *and the rats got scared!* They took one look at me and cowered in the corner. I scared the hell out of them." No matter what they tried, the rats froze. The sequence had to be reshot later in Los Angeles using "professional actor" rats.

Stone Pillow was a success. Lucy was happy to leave it at that, but Aaron Spelling came to Gary and told him that he thought it was time for Lucy to come back in a regular series. Lucy didn't want to do it.

Gary thought the idea of Lucy coming back in a weekly series was a good one. Lucy disagreed. She was too old to be playing

"Lucy," and she knew it. Aaron Spelling went to ABC and mentioned the idea of a new Lucy series, and the network made a firm offer on the spot. She wouldn't have to make a pilot, and the network would guarantee her a full season of twenty-two shows for top dollar. ABC would make Gary executive producer and pay him a large salary as well.

Gary contacted the old writers, as many of the old staff as was still around, and got a commitment from Gale Gordon to come back to work if Lucy said yes. Gary presented the whole package to her of Gale, Bob and Madelyn, Aaron Spelling, and himself. When she saw how much he wanted her to do it, she said yes. She knew right away she had made a mistake.

Once production started, Gary sensed that they were headed in the wrong direction. He wanted to approve all scripts and script changes, but the writers would "end run" him and go right to Lucy, whose heart wasn't in it to begin with. She didn't want fights. She just wanted to do the show and go home. Her "old oomph" was gone. She went along with everybody, and did what she was told.

She was photographed very carefully. The special lenses smoothed out her wrinkles well enough, but the camera couldn't hide the staleness of scripts or the fact that "Lucy" was too old to be acting the way she acted. In one episode, Lucy alphabetizes the contents of the hardware store so the items are easier to find. We didn't believe it for a minute. What was once funny now seemed stupid and embarrassing, and Lucy knew it.

After six weeks, ABC canceled the show because so few people were watching it. The ratings dropped so severely that the network felt Lucy would pull down the rest of the Saturday night lineup. Gary wanted to fight. He told the ABC people that the show could be fixed if they gave him a chance. He also begged them to try the show on a different night of the week, but they declined. They would rather take the substantial loss on *Life with Lucy* than go forward with it.

The only bright spot in the middle of the nightmare was working with Gale Gordon once again. She loved Gale very much, and thought he hadn't changed a bit since they rang down the curtain on their last series twelve years before. "Gale was the best sport in the world," Lucy said. "He'd try anything. Do anything we asked him to. He was always taking chances. He was eighty years old, and he could still turn a cartwheel."

It was more difficult for Lucy to talk about *Life with Lucy* than any other subject. She said she had never failed so royally in all her life, but she found it most hurtful that she disappointed so many people. She felt she had let her fans down because she was "doing crap," and she thought she let her staff down, the people who had been promised a year's worth of work and then had to be let go after six weeks.

The day they wrapped the show was one of the most traumatic of Lucy's life. She cried openly as she talked about it. "We walked out of the offices. I had a few scripts in my hand, and Gary was carrying a typewriter or something, and as we walked through the parking lot, people would turn away. Like we were lepers. Some of them looked like they wanted to say sorry, or something kind, but most of them looked at us and looked away. I felt like we were trying to sneak out without being seen. I felt like a thief carrying those things to the car. I felt like we were stealing. God, it was awful. I cried for three days," she said through her tears. "I guess I'm still crying about it."

About the same time, Lucy had more tears to shed when she learned that Desi had cancer and it was inoperable. Over the years,

Lucy and Desi remained close. In any interviews, they always spoke of each other with respect, love, and tenderness. Lucy still loved Desi, but more as a pal than an old lover. He joked with her on the phone that he was having chemotherapy, and it made all his white hair fall out. He had to wear a baseball cap to cover his head, or else he'd look like a Cuban Kojak.

Lucy wanted to go to Del Mar and see him, but he said no. He ordered her to stay away. She could call as often as she liked, and he encouraged that, but he wanted her to stay in Los Angeles. At first, she obeyed his orders, but when he took a turn for the worse, she went to see him despite his edict.

Even though Lucy was vain about the way she looked in public, she couldn't understand why Desi didn't want her to see what he looked like. He was very thin and sallow, and far from the dashing Latin lover who offered her rumba lessons some forty-six years before. Lucy talked to Desi through a closed door and begged him to let her in so she could say good-bye. Desi was firm. He wouldn't see her. He wanted her to remember him the way he was. But Lucy persisted and Desi relented. They had a long laugh-filled visit three weeks before he died.

Little Lucie went to Del Mar to take care of her father. Edie had died the year before, and aside from the occasional visits from his children, Desi was alone. Lucie visited her father more than Desi, Jr., did, and Lucy thought it was because he was unconsciously but deeply angry with his father. On more than one occasion, Lucy expressed her feelings that Desi, Jr., needed to forgive his father and get on with his life.

The call finally came. Desi was dead. After the funeral, Lucie Arnaz told her mother about Desi's last moments. She said she told her father that there was a bright white light waiting for him, and he must find it and go into it. God was waiting for him in the light. From the look on Desi's face, Lucie knows he saw it before he closed his eyes and died peacefully in her arms.

Lucy promised herself she would never work as an actress again. Gary wanted her to do a movie-of-the-week based on *The Solid Gold Cadillac*, but Lucy gave him a Bronx cheer when he suggested it.

"I can't top myself. So why should I try?"

She was offered another movie, called *The Story Lady*, about a grandmother who videotapes fairy tales for her grandchildren and becomes a celebrity when the videos become a big hit on television. Gary thought she should do it, but Lucy gave him another Bronx cheer.

I asked her to do my play, *The Lucky O'Learys*, and she gave *me* a Bronx cheer. The part of Peg, a woman who makes a deal with her favorite saint to win the biggest lottery in American history, was perfect for Lucy, but she didn't see herself in it.

"I can't play Irish," she protested.

"But she's Irish like *you're* English!"

"I don't care if she's a Spanish dancer, I don't want to do it."

I was surprised. "Don't you think it's good?"

"I think it's wonderful," she said. "I wouldn't want to produce it if I didn't think it was good. I just don't want to play the part. I don't want to play *any* part!" She took a deep breath when she said this, and then added, "I hope I don't jinx you."

I didn't understand. "How could you jinx me?"

She shook her head. "People don't care what I want to produce or direct or anything else. They just want to know if I want to be in it. And I don't. I don't want to be in anything."

She meant what she said about not wanting to be in anything, since she turned down a plum part in a remake of *Sweet Bird of Youth* that went to Elizabeth Taylor and asked the producers of *Driving Miss Daisy* *not* to consider her after an item appeared in a gossip column that she was actively lobbying for the part.

Still, she loved to make personal appearances in front of live audiences. She said yes to appearing at most of the tributes people wanted to give her, from the Museum of Broadcasting to the "Kennedy Center Honors." Lucy cried easily at these ceremonies, because the love that people showed overwhelmed her. None was more emotional than the night she was inducted into the Television Hall of Fame.

After a film clip of Lucy's historical career, Lucie Arnaz came on stage and sang a moving rendition of "I Love Lucy." At the end, she looked out front, and with her voice breaking said, "I love you, Mom." Lucy couldn't hold back the tears as she stepped up to the podium to accept the award. The mascara was running down her face in rivers as she finally managed to say a few words: "This tops 'em all!"

Lucy shook the dice and rolled. The front doorbell rang, but Lucy paid no attention as she made her move. If a stranger came to the door, he was to be told that "Miss Ball is not at home; she's working." Lucy continued playing as Frank walked to open the door. Then, as if her chair were electrified, Lucy jumped out of it. "Oh my God! I forgot!" She scared me half to death by jumping up. "What's the matter? What did you forget?"

"That's Tony Thomopolos! I forgot he was coming."

Tony Thomopolos is one of the most powerful men in the entertainment industry, as well as being one of the nicest. He has been president of ABC Entertainment, United Artists, and one of the people most responsible for *Rainman*. He is also married to TV talk-show host Christina Ferrare, whom Lucy adored. Lucy admired Christina for her self-made success after overcoming a lot of bad press. She also admired her as a mother who could balance work and raising happy and normal children at the same time.

Lucy grabbed her lipstick, broadly drew the famous arches over her upper lip, puckered, and blotted the rest with a cocktail napkin. She took a hand mirror and ran her fingers through her hair as Mr. Thomopolos was ushered into the foyer.

"Oh my God," she kept saying, "I can't believe I forgot he was coming over."

My mind started to race. If the great Thomopolos was coming to speak with the great Ball, it meant something big. Perhaps a triumphal return? A Broadway show? A new movie? I was getting excited as Lucy prepared to meet the producer, and I thought I was about to be privy to one of the biggest Hollywood deals of all time being put together. Tony came into the dining room smiling and holding out his arms to Lucy. He's a handsome man with an engaging personality, and Lucy welcomed him warmly. She introduced us and offered Tony some of her lemonade. I said, "I thought you liked this man. Why would you offer him your lousy lemonade?"

Thomopolos passed on the lemonade and got right down to business. He took a blue denim jacket out from under his arm and spread it across the dining-room table. On the back of the jacket was a large painting of Lucy's face with little rhinestones in her big blue eyes. She hopped back from the table. "Wow! Where did you get that?"

Tony told us that he had seen it in the Midwest, and he had bought it for Christina as a birthday surprise. Lucy laughed. "Is Christina going to wear it?"

Tony said, "No, I'm going to put it in plastic and hang it on the wall."

Lucy cocked her head. "In plastic on the wall? What does that mean?"

He meant they were going to frame it and light it.

Lucy clucked, "And I suppose you'll have the nerve to call it art?" Tony handed her a broad black magic marker, and she signed it, "To Christina, With Love, Lucy." Tony watched her like a little kid watching his favorite movie star signing his autograph book after a Saturday matinee.

Lucy handed the pen back to him and asked that he send her love back to Christina. He thanked her, gave her a kiss, and left. Lucy turned to me. "He's such a nice man. And she's the best. Come on, I owe you two bucks, and I want to get it back. Let's play."

As we sat back down at the table and set up the board, I was disappointed that Mr. Thomopolos came with a blue denim jacket for her to sign rather than a contract for a new movie starring Lucille Ball. But Lucy found more joy in the fact that a man who could buy and sell Hollywood found time to come across town to get an autograph for his wife.

CHAPTER
Twenty Two

APRIL 17, 1989, was a Monday. Lucy called to confirm our date, and I arrived at the house about one-thirty. As I walked up the driveway, I had no idea that this perfect California afternoon would be my last with Lucy.

She looked radiant. She wore a dark blue running suit, and around her neck the white silk scarf I had given her for Christmas. She had taken to wearing scarves or pearls after a thyroid operation a few years before. Although the surgery left an almost invisible scar, Lucy was very self-conscious about it. Her hair was done up, and she was bristling with energy.

Lucy was sitting in the corner of the den where she read, and she looked up when I came in. "Come here, I want you to look at this." She was holding a small book. It was very old, and the brittle brown pages cracked as she turned them. The book was one of a series of popular books for young girls, much like the Horatio Alger books were for boys.

"My grandmother gave me this," she said. "I used to read it over and over when I was a little girl. I've been looking for it for years, and it turned up in a drawer this morning. Funny, eh?"

I asked her what the book was about, and she said very unsentimentally, "You know. Same old stuff. A little girl has a dream, goes on a big adventure, and her dream comes true." It sounded to me like the life of Lucille Ball.

She showed me a picture that was taken at the Oscars. "I guess I don't look *too* frightening in this one."

I took the picture. It was terrific. I said, "You look great. Are you ready to talk about it yet?"

Lucy looked up at me, deciding if she was ready or not. She was very disappointed with herself at the 1989 Oscars, although everyone else thought she had been magnificent. Lucy didn't, and wouldn't discuss the appearance with me.

She had been looking forward to the Oscars for two months, and was very excited to be working with her dear pal Bob Hope. They had been asked to present the Oscar Winners of the Future. It was to be a symbol of the older generation of stars passing the baton to the younger.

About six weeks before the event, I came over to find Lucy looking at sketches of gowns that Ret Turner had designed for her. She lined them all up on the floor, and we looked at them. She liked an aqua chiffon gown with a high neck, but my eye went right to a black beaded dress with a silver sequin collar. I told her I liked it best, and she nonchalantly said, "Okay. I'll get that one." She placed the order but made Ret change the collar to gold beads to match her hair.

I met her the day she had her fitting, and she screamed at me, "I'm going to kill you! I just tried on that dress, and it weighs fifty pounds. It's a ton! I should have stayed with chiffon."

On the night of the Oscars, Lucy was a knockout. The dress looked sensational on her, and every time she took a step forward, a high-cut slit in the skirt revealed a long showgirl leg. When she and Bob Hope made their entrance, it was the most sustained ovation of the evening; the high point of the show. Lucy and Bob, who were movie stars before they ever went on television, were being acknowledged as living legends at the ultimate Hollywood event.

Gary and Lucy went to Irving Lazar's party at Spago afterward and sat with Michael Caine and his wife for a while, but Lucy was feeling tired and wanted to go home.

The next day all the papers singled out Lucy for being in top form and looking so glamorous. Lucy was not happy. When I saw her that day, she was very down.

"You were terrific last night."

Lucy shook her head. "No, I wasn't. I saw a tape of it. I was having trouble with my words and my teeth felt like they were too heavy and I looked just terrible and I don't want to talk about it."

I couldn't believe her negative reaction. "I think you and I were watching two different shows."

She was stern. "I said I don't want to talk about it."

Now, a few weeks later, she seemed ready to talk.

"Cary Grant wasn't gay, you know," she said.

"Where did that come from?" I asked.

"I was thinking about the night of the Oscars, and for some strange reason all I could think about was Cary Grant and all that trash that's coming out about him that isn't true. It's hard to believe that he's gone. He's still very much missed. You think of somebody as being around forever, and then they're gone. Everybody's gone. Hollywood's gone. It all hit me the night of the Oscars. Then I couldn't walk, I couldn't talk, my gums were hurting, my teeth were hurting. I can't do anything right anymore."

I told her I thought she was being too hard on herself.

She shook her head. "Nothing works. I look like a witch. I—"

"Stop it! It sounds like you want to punish yourself."

"I'm just disgusted. I can't drink. I can't smoke. I can't gamble. I can't drive. What have I got to look forward to?"

"Trouncing me at backgammon!"

She sighed, smiled, and slapped me on the knee. "You're right! Let's play," she said as she jumped from her chair. "I know something else we can look forward to," she said, heading to the kitchen, "I have a surprise for you." She opened the refrigerator door and pulled out a pitcher of lemonade.

"You gotta be kidding," I said. "That stuff is like cod liver oil on the rocks."

"Just taste it," she said with a cryptic smile.

I took a sip and swallowed. It was perfect; not too sweet, and just enough tang to refresh. "Excellent! How did you do it?"

"I followed your instructions, sir."

I took another sip as she put the pitcher back in the fridge and asked her, "Aren't you going to have a glass?" She closed the refrigerator door and said, "I already had some. It was horrible. Tasted like vinegar."

I choked on the gulp of lemonade I just took. I laughed so hard it went right up my nose. The lemonade was burning the inside of my nostrils, and Lucy thought it was the funniest thing she ever saw. She held on to the butcher-block table wailing with laughter as I screamed in pain.

She caught her breath and looked up at me. "You're funny."

I shook my head and said, "And so are you, lady!"

We walked to the backgammon table in a corner of the living room overlooking the backyard and sat down.

Lucy saw the large manila folder on top of the game board, and her mood changed immediately. Whenever Lucy's secretary, Wanda Clark, had papers for Lucy to look over or sign, she would send them to the house and they would be put on the back-gammon table to await Lucy's attention.

"I hate paperwork," she grunted as she took off the large paper clips. She opened the folder and looked through the contents. The top page was the itinerary of a forth-coming trip to the East Coast. Lucy had a strenuous trip in front of her. She was going to Jamestown to receive an honorary degree from Jamestown Community College of the State University of New York. She would then go on to Buffalo, where the Shea The-atre Chain was presenting her with the first annual Lucille Ball Award for outstanding people from the western New York State area. In Buffalo, they had also scheduled lunches, appearances, several press confer-ences, photo opportunities, and banquets that would keep her going for twelve hours a day for three days.

The day before her heart attack, Lucy was as strong and healthy as any seventy-seven-year-old woman could be. She had exercised in the morning with Onna White, and except for that "friggin' shoulder," she was in great shape.

She was looking forward to the trip back to her hometown but was apprehensive about the grueling schedule. She looked at the endless itinerary and sighed, "You give money to charity all your life, and then they punish you for it." She tossed aside the papers, saying that she would get to them the next day.

"I want Bobby," she said. I knew what that meant.

I put on her favorite album, *Bobby Darin Live at the Copa*. She knew every word, and often sang along in her low, gravelly voice, sounding more like Louie Armstrong than Lucille Ball.

Frank came in the room with a bouquet of flowers that had been sent by a fan, a minister in North Carolina. There was a note thanking Lucy for all the hours of happiness she had given the world. Her favorite flower was lilac, and this bouquet was full of them. On the bottom of his note was a North Carolina phone number. Lucy picked up the phone and dialed the number to thank the man personally. That's the way she was.

The minister was not home, but Lucy spoke to his wife and thanked her. The woman was obviously flabbergasted that she was talking to Lucille Ball, but Lucy spoke with her as though she were talking to an old friend. When Lucy put the phone down, she chuckled and said, "I wonder what she thinks about her husband sending flowers to another woman."

After a few games, Lucy's mood changed. She picked up the phone again. As she dialed, she told me she was calling Ruth Berle's mother, Sophie Rosenthal. Ruth, wife of Milton Berle, was recovering from cancer surgery at Cedars-Sinai.

"Hello, Sophie. It's Lucy." She didn't have to say anything else. She sat there with tears rolling down her face as Sophie told her that Ruth was in a coma and the prospects were very bad. (Ironically, Ruth Berle died only a few feet away from where Lucy was undergoing surgery the next day.)

When she finished the conversation, she left the room to wash her face. As she left the room, she sniffled and said, "It's so hard for a mother to outlive a child."

While Lucy was gone, I went to the dining room and looked through one of the scrapbooks. She kept everything. As I turned a page, a small card fell out of the book. It read, "Darling, I'm so sorry about last night. Love, Desi." I put the card back and closed the book, wondering what Desi was sorry about. I'd ask her about it tomorrow.

She came back and saw me looking

through the scrapbooks, and paused to look at them again. She said, "I'm a saver." She turned to the last page and found several copies of a publicity shot that was taken about the time she met Desi; a real glamour shot. Her hair is piled atop her head, and a white fur is draped over one shoulder. She said, "Do you have this one?"

"No, but I want it, and I want it now."

She signed it, put it in an envelope, and chuckled. "Pick it up on your way out."

We returned to the game table and started again. I was winning by eight points, and she was eager to catch up. She kept rolling the combination 6–4 over and over. After the fourth consecutive roll of 6–4 she shrugged and said, "This is the 'house of repeats.'"

After a while, Gary walked in. Lucy jumped up when she saw her husband and threw her arms around him. It was obvious Lucy adored him. Desi had been Lucy's heart-throb, but Gary was her soul mate. He could make Lucy laugh as no one else could, and to laugh a few times a day was what she lived for. He began lip-synching to Bobby Darin singing "Mack the Knife." Lucy howled as Gary threw in an unexpected bump.

Gary had to discuss business for a moment, and Lucy didn't like that. The following Monday, she was to be presented with the Kodak Life Achievement Award. Gary had requests for press conferences, most of which he turned down, a few he couldn't.

Lucy interrupted him. "No cameras!"

Gary implored, "Honey, there has to be cameras."

"No, I don't want to be photographed."

Gary continued, "There's no getting around it. They're going to be taking your picture when they give you the award."

Lucy was getting desperate, and she blew her top. "Why are they giving me this award? I don't even know what it's for."

Gary was calming. "They're giving you this award for developing young talent. You deserve it. It's going to be a very nice affair, and they're even going to give us a free lunch. Isn't that nice of them?"

Lucy was starting to smile. "I don't know why they want to take pictures."

Gary threw up his arms in mock exasperation. "Why do they want to take pictures? This is the Kodak Company, Lucy. They don't want to give you a salami."

Lucy laughed. Gary won. He danced out of the room and upstairs to change. Lucy and I played a few more games. She was getting tired but was energized by the fact that she was whipping me good. When I announced "last game" at four-thirty, I didn't realize it would be our last game forever.

She won. I paid off my debt to her, $1.75. She walked me through the living room and looked up at me. "Don't forget your picture."

"I won't."

"Will I see you tomorrow?" she asked.

"You sure will," I replied. "Same time, same station."

She picked up the manila envelope from the TV set and handed it to me. I took the envelope and thought about the day I ran down the aisle for her autograph some thirty years before at the matinee of *Wildcat* and she said, "No autographs today." I started down the hallway not knowing that I was holding the last autograph Lucille Ball would ever sign.

"See you tomorrow, Lucy," I called over my shoulder.

"Drive safely," she shouted.

I turned back and looked at her framed in the doorway. The light was behind her, giving a flame glow to her orange-red hair. She looked beautiful.

I don't know what made me walk back to her and hold her for a moment, but I did. I kissed her on the cheek and noticed how clear and porcelain her skin was . . . like a young girl's.

I headed down the hallway again and got to the door. She shouted out in a twangy voice, "Good-bye, baby!" I shouted back "Good-bye, baby!" blew her a kiss, and closed the door behind me.

The next day, I called her at ten-thirty. Gary's nephew Michael answered the phone and told me Lucy wasn't available. He was trying to be nonchalant, but I got the feeling something was wrong. I told him I would be over at one-thirty as usual, and he said that would be fine. Lucy would see me then.

I called back at noon. I wanted to talk to Lucy. Michael told me that Gary had just taken her to the hospital. They didn't think it was serious. They thought she was hyperventilating.

Lucy had awakened early but stayed in bed. About 10:00 A.M., she called down for her breakfast. Seconds later, she called again, unable to breathe and barely able to talk. Chris, Roza, and Frank ran upstairs to the bedroom. Frank phoned the doctor, who asked him to take Lucy's blood pressure. Frank was shocked at how low it was, but didn't want to tell the doctor in front of Lucy. He said he couldn't find it.

An ambulance was called, and Gary got a phone call in his car to turn around and come home immediately.

Lucy was still reluctant to go to the hospital. She thought she was having an angina attack, and it would pass. When she finally agreed to go, she wouldn't leave the house until she had put on her makeup.

When they arrived at the emergency room of Cedars-Sinai, the doctors knew immediately that Lucy was in a life-threatening situation. Her aorta was ripping, and if she didn't have an emergency transplant immediately, she would die.

Amazingly, a donor was found, and Lucy underwent almost nine hours of surgery. It was tremendously successful. She was awake the next morning at nine forty-five, asking if Tinker was all right. When Gary arrived, she asked him if the surgery was serious, and he told her it was. She closed her eyes and nodded. "I know."

When Lucie Arnaz got to see her mother, Lucy was trying to say something to her through the oxygen mask. Lucie leaned over but still couldn't make out what her mother was trying to tell her. She carefully lifted the oxygen mask, and Lucy whispered in her ear, "Wouldn't you know? Today was the day I was supposed to have my hair dyed."

Lucy progressed amazingly well. She was out of bed two days after the surgery, and walked on the next. The doctors moved her out of intensive care into a cardiac unit. I spoke to Gary on the evening of April 25, and he was very upbeat. Lucy would be able to see me in two days, and then she'd be home in about a week. I was very happy. I knew she'd come back.

As I was watching the CBS *Morning News* the next day, the program was interrupted for a special report. I couldn't imagine what it was. The voice was blunt. "Actress Lucille Ball has died in Los Angeles. She was seventy-seven when she succumbed to a fatal heart attack at five o'clock this morning, Los Angeles time. We now continue with our regularly scheduled program."

The phone rang almost immediately, as it continued to do all day. I had more condolence calls the day Lucy died than I did at the time of my own father's death. In the afternoon, my friend Steve and I drove past Lucy's house, where we had spent so many happy hours. There were guards in front of every door and at the end of the driveway. Across the street was a large crowd of fans who stood silently looking at the house. A "Grave-Line" hearse giving a tour of dead movies stars' homes passed by. Lucy's had already been added. We decided to drive on.

We went to Hollywood Boulevard and found Lucy's star on the sidewalk. People were staring at it and weeping openly. Someone had placed a string of rosary beads on it, next to a rose. People who hadn't heard the news stopped to see what was going on. All the people reacted as if they had just been told of a death in their own family.

I talked to Trudi, who was with Lucy when she died on April 26, 1989. She told me Lucy woke up about ten to five with a pain in her back. A moment later, she lost consciousness and died. The lower part of her aorta had ruptured. Trudi told me that no matter what we heard about Lucy getting better, the surgery would have debilitated her tremendously, and she would never have been the same.

The day after Lucy died, her body was cremated. On Friday, Frank drove Gary, who was carrying Lucy's ashes, to the Forest Lawn cemetery in the Hollywood Hills. About one o'clock, he buried them, he and Lucy alone together for the last time. A few hours later, Lucie and Desi, Jr., came with their families to say good-bye to their mother.

Lucy left specific wishes as to what she wanted for a memorial service—a family picnic like the ones she remembered as a little girl in Jamestown. She left a list of what she wanted served, including ham, baked beans, potato salad, watermelon: all the things she remembered from her childhood. When I heard that Lucy insisted lemonade be served, I wondered if she hadn't done it just to get the last laugh.

The picnic was held on Mother's Day at the old home of the late Robert Taylor in Mandeville Canyon. I brought Steve Schalchlin and Hal King. Security was heavy around the picnic area; they didn't want the *National Enquirer* there. Wanda Clark stood at the front gate to identify everyone going in.

About fifty people were there: Lucy's inner circle, including Lee Tannen, Audrey Meadows, Mary Wickes, Onna White, Paula Stewart, Thelma Orloff, Lorna Luft, and

Lucy's TV daughter Ann Dusenberry. Lucie and Larry's ex-spouses, Phil Vandervort and Robin Strasser, were both there, which everyone agreed was very civilized.

The only person missing was Lucy. To have so many reminders of her around and not have her was making everyone misty. We were all laughing as we sat around the table telling Lucy stories, but the laughter was hollow. We all secretly hoped she would climb out on a window ledge and say, "Ha-ha. Fooled you. I was just having fun."

Bobby Darin's Copa album was playing through the speakers. He was singing a very hip version of "Swing Low, Sweet Chariot." I couldn't take any more. I was going to cry.

I got home about three in the afternoon and flipped on the television. Before the picture came on, I broke into tears and sat there sobbing as the realization was finally sinking in that my friend was gone and I couldn't play with her anymore. Suddenly, I heard her voice saying, "Well, really!," and I looked up at the screen. *I Love Lucy* faded in. It was the episode where Lucy and Ethel have chosen the same dress to wear for a charity performance, and sing a duet of "Friendship!" They both refuse to take their dresses back, and end up ripping each other apart.

I was crying so much I felt as if I were watching the episode under water. But as Lucy and Ethel started to sing, I started to smile. By the time they were tearing the cabbage roses off each other's skirts, I was laughing. When they finished the number, I was howling. Lucy had done what she did so many times before—turned tears into laughter. I felt lucky to have known her and thankful for her friendship.

I miss spending time with her more than anything in the world, but I find comfort knowing that as long as there are TV sets and memories, I will always have Lucy in the afternoon.

Epilogue

A FEW WEEKS later, I had a dream about her. I was sitting at home when my friend Mort came into the room and said, "Lucy's waiting for you."

I didn't appreciate the bad joke. "What are you talking about?" I said. "Lucy's dead."

"Just go down the hall and to the left," he said.

I got up and found a long corridor. I walked through the hall until I got to the last door on the left. There was a gold star on the door, and engraved in the star, LUCILLE BALL.

I knocked on the door and heard her call to me. "Jim?"

"Yes, Lucy."

"Well, it's about time. Come on in!"

I opened the door and saw Lucy standing by a huge picture window bathed in light. She was all in white, the same as the first day I spent with her. She was Lucy in her later years but glorified, radiant and golden. She put her hand on her hip and said, "Hi, honey. I thought you'd never get here."

I was furious with her. "Why are you doing this?" I asked. "The whole world is upset. Everybody thinks you're dead. I don't think this is funny."

She laughed. "*You're* funny. I just wanted to tell you I'll be around. I'll see you. We'll be in touch."

I could feel the tears welling up in my eyes. "Can't I stay with you?" I asked.

"Don't be silly! You have too much to do.

And don't start blubbering, either!" she warned me.

"Lucy . . . I love you."

"You, too, kiddo. Good-bye, baby!"

I had to ask her. "Why did you die?"

Lucy looked me in the eye and said, "I didn't want to go to Buffalo."

End of dream. End of story.